LEARNING DIFFICULTIES

LEARNING DIFFICULTIES

Causes and Psychological Implications—
A Guide for Professionals

By

KURT GLASER, M.D., M.Sc.

Associate Professor in Pediatrics and
Assistant Clinical Professor in Psychiatry
University of Maryland School of Medicine
Assistant Professor in Pediatrics
Johns Hopkins University School of Medicine
Consultant, Central Evaluation Clinic for Children
University of Maryland Hospital
Consultant, Departments of Psychiatry and Pediatrics
Sinai Hospital of Baltimore
Director, Adolescent Services
Springfield Hospital Center

Assisted by

Susanne Glaser, M.S.W.

With a Foreword by

Leo Kanner, M.D.

CHARLES C THOMAS · PUBLISHER
Springfield · Illinois · U.S.A.

Published and Distributed Throughout the World by
CHARLES C THOMAS • PUBLISHER
Bannerstone House
301-327 East Lawrence Avenue, Springfield, Illinois, U.S.A.

© *1974, by* CHARLES C THOMAS • PUBLISHER
ISBN 0-398-03157-6
Library of Congress Catalog Card Number: 74-3257

With THOMAS BOOKS *careful attention is given to all details of
manufacturing and design. It is the Publisher's desire to present books
that are satisfactory as to their physical qualities and artistic possibilities
and appropriate for their particular use.* THOMAS BOOKS *will be true
to those laws of quality that assure a good name and good will.*

Printed in the United States of America
W-2

Library of Congress Cataloging in Publication Data

Glaser, Kurt, 1915-
    Learning difficulties; causes and psychological
implications—a guide for professionals.

    Bibliography: p.
    1. Handicapped children—Education. I. Glaser,
Susanne, joint author. II. Title. [DNLM: 1. Learning
disorders. 2. Psychology, Educational. LB1051 G548L
1974]
LC4015.G54   371.9'1   74-3257
ISBN 0-398-03157-6

FOREWORD

Dr. John C. Whitehorn, the eminent American psychiatrist, has summed up the function of a specialty with great wisdom. He wrote: "The medical profession, in its general progress to gain better health for its people, improves the rate and sureness of its progress by a division of scholarly and investigative labor, whereby some devote themselves to special problems, to the expert development of special methods, with the ultimate aim of solving these problems in a manner to increase the effectiveness of all the medical professions. . . . In this sense a specialty is an extensive investigative task force whose task is to bring a special health area under better knowledge and control. The specialist is particularly dedicated to spoiling his field of expertness by such a radical resolution of the uncertainties and misunderstandings in that field as to make a high degree of expertness in certain areas less necessary than before." In the area of child welfare this means that the professional experts should assume the obligation to transmit their insights to all those responsible for the health and education of children.

This formulation is highly applicable to the work done by Dr. Kurt Glaser, as deposited in this volume.

The author, thoroughly familiar with the investigative labor of experts in the field of learning difficulties, has undertaken the task of summarizing, condensing and elucidating the insights gained thus far so that they may become available to the nonexpert.

In many scientific fields, we can see a similar historical sequence. Out of vague diffusion, a circumscribed set of facts is isolated and studied in great detail. It thus becomes a specialty and thereby the exclusive domain of a select group of experts. As time goes on, it becomes apparent that the new knowledge cannot be contained in a tight capsule. The facts can be seen as having different relations with knowledge obtained in different areas and invite collaboration with specialists in other fields. Finally, the matter seeps through to the general public, which needs and should gain admittance to the progress made, so that it can be utilized practically in everyday living.

This is precisely what has happened in the area of learning difficulties. The very concept, as we use it now, is very recent and covers less than a century. Since its nascency, clusters of building stones were carried together from pediatrics, neurology, psychiatry, pedagogy, psychology and sociology to be housed in one large edifice, the special study of learning difficulties. Many learned treatises attest to the wealth of theory, research and practical application.

It is good to have someone with actual clinical experience come along and present a readable distillation of the existing knowledge to everyone, not necessarily a learning difficulty expert, who has active interest in the health and education of children and adolescents. Dr. Glaser has superbly succeeded in letting the reader in on the available knowledge, communicating actual facts, shying away from confusing phraseology and from unchecked theorizing. The "expert" can still benefit from this book as a guiding syllabus, but its greatest usefulness will be derived by pediatricians, educators, social workers and interested parents.

LEO KANNER, M.D.
Professor Emeritus
Honorary Consultant
The Johns Hopkins University
School of Medicine

PREFACE

THE PURPOSE OF this book is to provide the reader with a guide to various causes of learning disorders and their interaction, with special emphasis on the impact of psychological factors, both as causes and consequences. It is directed toward all professionals who work with children in the fields of education and health care, and it might also be of help to educated parents.

The author's intent is to help bridge the gap between the views and approaches of various professional disciplines with regard to causative influences upon the functioning and development of the child. Everyone involved with children can enhance their well-being by a greater understanding of all the factors which may affect the learning process and by an awareness of how learning difficulties, in turn, may have an impact upon the total development of the child.

Much of the experience for the content of this book and the preceding articles (which are listed in the bibliography) has been gained from patients seen in private practice and from the many years as psychiatric consultant at the Central Evaluation Clinic for Children of the University of Maryland Hospital. I wish to express my appreciation to Dr. Raymond Clemmens, Director of the Central Evaluation Clinic for Children, for providing the opportunity for close collaboration with all staff members of the Clinic. The many open and challenging discussions during our Clinic conferences have provided a background for the formulation of many of the thoughts expressed in this book.

My special thanks go to Dr. Leo Kanner, for his guidance throughout the years and for reviewing the manuscript and making many valuable suggestions.

Some paragraphs from earlier papers by the author have been used in this book with the permission of Dr. Raymond Clemmens and the editors of *Pediatrics* and the *American Journal of Psychotherapy*.

KURT GLASER, M.D.

INTRODUCTION

It is no longer acceptable to ignore the child who does not perform in school, to let him drop behind or leave school altogether. Job opportunities for those with inadequate education, especially with insufficient reading skills, have diminished and continue to become scarcer. Jobs traditionally performed by uneducated people are disappearing: the farm hand is replaced by the operator of farm machinery; the street cleaner by the driver of sophisticated cleaning trucks; the maid is expected to operate household machines and comprehend and transmit telephone messages; the gas station attendant must be able to read manuals of the many, annually changing models of cars in order to perform even the simplest maintenance jobs. While industrialization created many unskilled assembly line jobs, automation has been rapidly reducing and replacing them. The acquisition of knowledge and skills has become a necessity for survival in our culture where reading is a basic tool for learning.

There is no evidence that the incidence of learning disabilities has increased in recent years, but awareness of the significance of the problem certainly has risen sharply. Instead of waiting for school failure to occur, educators now look for the child with potential learning disability, recognize shortcomings earlier, and discover milder cases which in the past were overlooked. It has become the task of all educators and health professionals to find, treat, and correct learning disabilities or, better yet, to prevent their occurrence.

There have been expectations of major medical breakthroughs which would reduce or prevent damage in those children whose learning difficulties are due to organic defects. It is true that prenatal, perinatal, and postnatal damage has been reduced; that improved prenatal care is available to larger numbers of women;

that reduction of birth trauma and improved health care have reduced morbidity and the production of damaged children. But it is equally true that the decrease in infant mortality has resulted in an increased survival rate of infants who are high at risk for the development of difficulties, including learning problems, in later life. The weak and/or damaged infant who will need additional services throughout childhood and, in some cases, throughout life has a greater chance of survival. Our ability to save some premature infants and children with congenital heart or lung defects are examples of medical progress which reduces infant mortality and increases the survival rate of the high-risk child.

Many professional disciplines are interested and involved in the field of learning disabilities. Educators—whether classroom teachers, curriculum planners, researchers, or administrators—are, of course, in the forefront. But social workers, psychologists, speech and language clinicians, psychiatrists, pediatricians, neurologists, otologists, ophthalmologists, optometrists, and other health professionals are often essential to complete the team. Depending on the cause, the child's age, and accidental factors, one of these specialists is likely to be the first to recognize the defect or a predisposing factor. In the very young it is the physician who is in a position to recognize visual or auditory defects and thus initiate corrective measures and forestall future difficulties. Later it is most likely the educator who first calls attention to an abnormality which may interfere with learning.

Precise diagnosis and subsequent treatment may or may not be in the direct province of the teacher and may require the collaboration of all team members to identify the defect(s), map out a course of action, and guide the child and his family through the frequently complex process of remediation. But recognition of the cause of the learning disability usually points the way toward a course of treatment and/or preventive measures needed to improve the condition or avoid further damage.

It is the purpose of this book to discuss various causes of learning disabilities in order to provide guidance in diagnosis, prevention, and treatment to those engaged in the education and health care of children. Brief specific references will be made to treatment where indicated, and some controversies about therapeutic procedures will be dealt with.

For the purpose of this discussion the term Learning Difficulty is considered in the broadest sense. It encompasses any problem in scholastic performance, whether cause or consequence, whether organic, emotional, or educational, whether specific in one field or subject (e.g. reading) or general (e.g. underachieving), whether occurring in the young child just beginning his school career or in the adolescent toward the end of obligatory school attendance. It includes learning problems due to such organic factors as defective vision or hearing, or minimal brain dysfunction, or to entities of as yet uncertain etiology such as specific reading disability or dyslexia. Social and cultural factors as well as psychological disturbances and educational factors contributing to school failure will be discussed. However, learning problems associated with gross physical or psychiatric deviations, including manifest brain damage with obvious neurological defects such as cerebral palsy, seizures or mental retardation, severe visual or auditory abnormalities or psychotic disorders (infantile autism, childhood schizophrenia) will be dealt with only incidentally. Such conditions are usually recognized without difficulty before school entrance and special educational programs are often available for these children.

Particular emphasis will be placed on multifactorial influences and the reciprocal effect of learning disorders and emotional factors. Learning disorders from any cause may have disturbing psychological effects, and the emotional consequences may, in turn, interfere with the learning process and may make correction of the defect more difficult. Truancy and school phobia may be a cause or a consequence of learning difficulties. Social, psychological, or educational factors may have induced a child to absent himself from school, and the absence will have educational and psychological consequences. Eisenberg (1966) states that "psychopathology is a frequent concomitant of retardation in reading," and in many cases ". . . the psychiatric disorder is the source of the reading problem." On the other hand, ". . . it must be recognized that the reading difficulty is in itself a potent source of emotional distress."

The literature on learning difficulties is voluminous and often deals with specific entities or single studies and individual points of view. This treatise is attempting to provide the reader with an overview of the multitude of causes and related treatment procedures, with special emphasis on the interaction of psychological causes and sequelae.

CONTENTS

Page

Foreword—Leo Kanner v

Preface vii

Introduction ix

Chapter

I. Physical Factors 3

    Visual and Auditory Handicaps 3

    Chronic Illness, Deficiencies, and Defects 5

    Speech and Language Disorders 6

    Maturational Lag 6

    Minimal Brain Dysfunction 8

    Genetic Factors and Specific Reading Disability 16

II. Intelligence and Learning Difficulties 22

    Assessment of Intelligence 22

    Mild Mental Retardation 25

    Relative Retardation 26

    Relative Intellectual Superiority 29

III. Environmental Factors 32

    The Home Influence 32

        Family Mobility 32

        Competitiveness 33

        Low Motivation 34

        Economic Factors 37

        Parental Neglect 37

        Distracting Factors 38

        Deprivation 38

    Cultural Influence 39

        Social Pressure 39

        Psychological Impact of Cultural Factors 40

        Wandering Youth 41

        Shift of Values 41

Chapter   *Page*
        Rebellion Against Categorization 42
        Drug Abuse 42
   IV. PSYCHOLOGICAL FACTORS 44
        Stress Unrelated to the Learning Process 44
            Domestic Conflict 45
            Changes in Family Composition 45
            Physical Conditions Leading to Psychological Stress 46
            Individuation and Separation (School Phobia) 48
        Conflicts Related to the Learning Process 51
            Truancy and Delinquency 51
            Negativism and Rebellion 54
            Frustration and Healthy Curiosity 55
            Negative Influences (Interpersonal Reactions) 56
        Major Psychiatric Disorders 57
            Schizophrenia 57
            Depression 60
    V. EDUCATIONAL FACTORS 62
        Open-Space Classroom 62
        Homogeneous Versus Heterogeneous Grouping
            (Ability Grouping) 63
        Social Promotion 64
        Early Detection and Remediation 65
   VI. THE ROLE OF THE PROFESSIONAL 68
  VII. GLIMPSES INTO THE FUTURE 72
        Neurochemistry 73
        Maturation and School Onset 74
        Values, Industrialization, Automation, and
            Economic Motivation 76
            Values 76
            Industrialization and Automation 77
            Economic Motivation 78
        Simplification of Language 79
        Expansion of Preventive Measures 80

Bibliography 82
Index 87

LEARNING   DIFFICULTIES

CHAPTER I

PHYSICAL FACTORS

A CHILD WHO HAS academic or behavioral difficulties in school may well have a physical handicap interfering with optimal functioning.

VISUAL AND AUDITORY HANDICAPS

Educators have long recognized that mild visual and auditory handicaps may go undiscovered prior to school entrance. A child who has never experienced normal sensory input has no standards of comparison and therefore cannot recognize any deviance until he is exposed to the structured setting of the school and is observed as not being able to see, hear, or perform like his peers. He experiences frustration, often without being aware of its cause.

Most parents will not recognize sensory defects in the preschool years unless these are relatively severe. The physician often sees the child only at the time of an acute illness. Even during routine checkups, not all physicians extend their examination to include tests for the discovery of relatively minor yet handicapping sensory disorders. For this reason many schools have established their own vision and hearing screening tests for all children.

In some instances the correction of sensory defects may be all that is needed to ameliorate the learning difficulty and restore self-confidence. In others, however, damage has already occurred which may require specific psychological or educational correction. The child may have been sufficiently deprived of visual and

3

auditory stimuli from early infancy, so that at age five or six he enters the structured learning process with less experiential information than his peers. He has experienced frustration, disappointment, and inability to compete with his peers or gain approval from parents or school personnel. He may react by withdrawing, underachieving, daydreaming, lack of interest, or he may try to regain status by attention-getting mechanisms such as clowning or assertion through aggressiveness. These behavior deviations are often interpreted as laziness, poor upbringing, or meanness. It is not always easy for the teacher to relate inappropriate behavior to a physical defect, especially if the behavior, having been practiced for some time, continues to persist after the correction of the defect by glasses or hearing aid.

The severity of the emotional impact of physical defects in the young child cannot be measured or predicted readily, as much depends on factors other than sensory deprivation. The family structure and the support and stimulation obtained in the preschool years, as well as the dynamics and constitutional characteristics of the child, will determine his resilience to noxious influences. In many cases the child with early stimulus deprivation may need special educational assistance, speech and language therapy, or psychiatric help, even after the correction of the defect. Prevention of deprivation and of psychological effects through early screening procedures and corrective measures is obviously desirable.

There is little doubt that handicaps related to acuity of vision and of sufficient severity will interfere with learning and should be corrected by lenses at the earliest possible moment. Some optometrists claim that since visual perceptual abilities are necessary for effective reading, optometric vision training programs will correct learning dysfunction. They further claim that developmental vision training programs will enhance the child's reading readiness.

A most extensive review of the subject by B. K. Keogh in 1973 reaches the conclusion that research results to date are not conclusive to justify these claims. While it is possible to interpret reading as a function of good visual perceptual ability, it is equally possible to reason that, as the child learns to read, he develops adequate visual perceptual organization, he masters scanning in a horizontal left to right direction, and he learns how to control his eyes in a coordinated fashion. Controlled objective studies are needed to show the efficacy of orthoptic developmental training in either enhancing reading readiness or correcting reading dysfunctions.

So far studies have shown that there is no peripheral eye defect which produces dyslexia and associated learning disabilities, according to a Joint Organizational Statement by the American Academy of Pediatrics, the American Academy of Ophthalmology and Otolaryngology, and the American Association of Ophthalmology (*Pediatrics,* 1972). Until and unless proof of efficacy is forthcoming, children should not be exposed to costly and time-consuming procedures. False hope and subsequent disappointment as well as delay in the initiation of other remedial processes can have detrimental effects upon the child's psychological adjustment as well as learning process. Goldberg, an ophthalmologist who has done extensive studies on the role of vision in learning, suggests that the educator, after identifying the deficit, "proceed to teach around the deficit, so that years of frustration are not allowed to ensue." (Goldberg & Schiffman, 1972).

CHRONIC ILLNESS, DEFICIENCIES, AND DEFECTS

Other organic pathological conditions may reduce the child's energy and interfere with his ability to concentrate on a sustained learning process. Malnutrition, anemia, glandular malfunctions, or other chronic diseases may go undetected until the child's unexplained scholastic malfunctioning suggests a thorough investigation of his physical condition. The damage sustained by the delayed learning process may need specific remediation even after removal of its organic underlying cause.

The physician must play a pivotal role in the detection, treatment, and correction of physical disorders. He as well as other professional personnel must, however, be acutely aware that both physical and psychological factors in the presence of a learning disability may, but do not have to be causatively related to the learning difficulty. They can be unrelated and noncontributory, or may be a consequence of the educational handicap and/or secondarily contributory. For example, a squint (cross-eyedness), or nearsightedness, or a psychological problem such as enuresis may exist and have no effect on the learning process. Thus treatment, even though desirable for cosmetic or other reasons, will not alter the unrelated learning disability. Or, shyness, anxiety states, or other problems may be the consequence rather than the cause of learning disorders. Finally, a learning disorder due to visual defects may cause psychological problems which in turn may aggravate the learning problem and thus create an escalating reciprocal cycle.

Chronic fatigue and hunger may interfere with a child's ability to learn. They may occur in the low socioeconomic group but are also seen in the well-to-do as a result of poor living habits.

SPEECH AND LANGUAGE DISORDERS

Speech and language problems not only interfere with effective communication, essential for the learning process, but they also have a profound psychological and social impact. Early therapeutic intervention is necessary to reduce or avoid their impact on the child's functioning at school.

MATURATIONAL LAG

Problems in academic achievement and behavioral adjustment are far more common in boys than in girls. It is generally assumed that social pressures, child rearing practices, and educational expectations centering around the role of the male in our society are the primary causative factors for this predominance of problems in boys.

However, as Bentzen (1963) has pointed out, organic factors may play at least an equally important role. It is well documented that the human male matures more slowly than the female. While the rate of maturation of sexual and bone development can be measured readily, practical methods of measuring maturational rates of the central nervous system are lacking.

Within the same sex group the onset of developmental processes, like other human characteristics, is distributed along the Gaussian frequency distribution curve. Thus reading readiness, motor ability, and speech and language development may vary greatly from child to child without being abnormally delayed or accelerated. For instance, reversals of letters and numbers are normally expected in the preschool child and disappear gradually during the first three grades. Their disappearance is necessary for effective reading and writing.

Wetzel *et al.* showed in 1971 that a Bender Gestalt Test administered to seven-year-olds and scored by the Koppitz Scoring System provided findings considered to indicate brain dysfunction. This test repeated one year later on the same children showed negative results in a substantial number. The findings indicate that these children were not brain damaged but simply matured at a slower rate.

The compulsory onset of schooling in this country is tied to a fixed date—September of the year in which the child has his sixth birthday. At this point children are expected to be ready to learn reading and writing. However, within each class there are chronological age differences of as much as twelve months, in addition to the developmental difference between girls and boys and individual differences in each sex group. We may thus find in one class a young male child, with a slower developmental maturational rate, sitting next to an older girl in a considerably more advanced maturational phase. It is plausible to hypothesize that the boy may undergo considerable stress in his attempt to keep up with the learning process, while the girl may be bored.

To cope with this discrepancy in readiness levels we would either have to have very small heterogeneous classes, where each child could be taught at his own rate, or schools large enough to have homogeneously grouped parallel classes on each grade level. The establishment of staggered entrance dates may be another possibility to be considered.

Any of these or other approaches, however, may create additional problems. For instance, youngsters in the heterogeneously grouped class may feel hurt by the constantly evident higher achievement of children of his own age; the child in the homogeneously grouped class may be stigmatized by being in the "dummy class" or become arrogant because of his placement in a higher class; school entrance at different age levels may present problems of social and physical maturity.

Obviously there are no easy answers to this very complex and crucial situation. But it seems essential that those working with this particular age group be aware of the wide variability in maturational rates.

MINIMAL BRAIN DYSFUNCTION

The realization that behavior, language, and learning problems can be caused by minimal central nervous system disorders, in the absence of overt evidence of mental retardation or neuromotor impairment, has come about only gradually in the recent past, and much about the subject still remains controversial. This syndrome has been described under various titles such as minimal brain damage, minimal brain or cerebral dysfunction, hyperkinetic syndrome, hyperkinetic impulse disorder, or minimal chronic brain syndrome.

Much of the current interest in this field can be attributed to the works of Goldstein (1939) and Strauss and Lehtinen (1950), who were interested in the educational rehabilitation of this group of children. Originally the same symptoms had been observed in grossly brain damaged and retarded youngsters. They believed that the disturbed functioning of these children was a result of organic impairment. Pasamanick and Lilienfeld (1956), Kawi and Pasamanick (1959), and Drillien (1961, 1963) demonstrated the correlation between pregnancy and perinatal complications on one hand, and certain learning and behavior disorders on the other. In 1964 Birch made a thorough review of the then available material on the subject which was published as an extensive annotated bibliography.

The group of children we are dealing with manifests, in the presence of at least average intelligence, hyperkinesis, impulsivity, short attention span, distractibility, perseveration, concreteness of thought, visuomotor discoordination, and, almost universally, learning and language difficulties. These children are temperamentally unstable, exhibit little capacity to tolerate stress and have difficulty in adjusting to and achieving in a regular classroom setting (Glaser and Clemmens, 1965). Their inability to exclude extraneous stimuli (distractibility) makes them particularly vulnerable in such recent educational ventures as open-spaced classrooms.

Hyperkinesis, a constant, seemingly aimless moving about, was described by Kahn and Cohen in 1934 who coined the term "organic drivenness." Leo Kanner describes such children as trying to control their built-in motor and being unable to find the clutch.

That a neurological defect exists is further supported by findings in the expanded neurological examination. While gross neurological signs are absent by definition, so-called soft or equivocal signs should be found in every child labeled brain-damaged. Some of these signs are: awkwardness, especially in fine motor activities such as buttoning a shirt, tying shoes, or standing or hopping on one foot; fine tremors in the fingers when arms are held outstretched; inability to turn hands rapidly and symmetrically; and mildly asymmetrical and hyperactive tendon reflexes. These children frequently have difficulty in differentiating left from right, have articulation disorders, and the occurrence of strabismus is more frequent (Clemmens and Glaser, 1967). The diagnosis of central nervous system dysfunction can be supported further by deviations from the norm in psychological tests such as the Bender Gestalt, positive electroencephalographic findings, and a confirmatory pregnancy and birth history (Goldberg and Schiffman, 1972; Money, 1962).

Such children have difficulties in learning to read and write in spite of average or superior overall intellect and competent instruction over adequate periods of time with pedagogical methods which succeed in most children.

It is not our intent to comment on the controversy in nomenclature or the polemic on the presence or absence, type or degree of organic damage or deficit or its possible causes. May it suffice to mention that minimal brain dysfunction may be caused by perinatal illness or injury (sustained before, during, or after birth) interfering with normal cerebral development. It may be the result of biochemical (enzymatic) irregularities and possibly genetic factors, although the latter group may constitute a separate entity (see Specific Reading Disability). Future research may allow us to divide the syndrome of minimal brain dysfunction more specifically in terms of size and location of lesions, etiology, prevention, and maybe even treatment.

In 1924 Gerstmann described an interesting syndrome of finger agnosia (inability to identify and locate the position of one's fingers), disorientation in directionality (right and left confusion), agraphia (inability to write), and acalculia (inability to calculate). Its specificity for a local lesion in the parietal occipital area was emphasized by him in 1940. Gerstmann thought that the syndrome, now named after him, would probably be found more frequently if looked for in children with learning disabilities. Hermann and Norrie (1958) considered that dyslexia and the Gerstmann syndrome may have a similar origin in a disturbance of directional functions. Prechtl (1962), while looking for a "uniform neurological syndrome" in these hyperkinetic children, discovered in a significant number the occurrence of choreiform movements associated with poor reading performance. The occurrence of these jerky, irregular, and arrhythmical movements in different muscles was confirmed by Wolff and Hurwitz (1966) and by Rutter and coworkers (1966).

Injuries to the brain during later years of childhood, while the brain is still in the formative stages (car accidents, lead intoxication, falls or illnesses such as encephalitis and meningitis) may also be the cause of the syndrome of minimal brain dysfunction, although these traumata will often produce clearly diagnosable neurological deficits and would not be categorized as "minimal." Some already available social and medical preventative approaches are obvious, but current knowledge is unfortunately not applied to the fullest extent (e.g. car accidents and seat belts, lead poisoning and paint).

Behavioral characteristics of the hyperkinetic child (hyperkinesis, short attention span, inability to concentrate, and lack of impulse control) are believed to be organically derived, but complications resulting from these symptoms and their effects upon the child and his environment will further alter the behavior and interfere with the ability to function adequately.

The child with hyperkinesis may have been a disappointment to his parents from early infancy. Expecting a placid, easily tractable baby, the mother finds a squirming, irritable infant who is unusually sensitive to sound and other stimuli. As a toddler he is always on the go; in nursery school he does not complete his tasks and disturbs the orderly process of the group by running, climbing and always being in motion. He is unable to stay within the lines when coloring pictures and moves erratically from one activity to the next without completing anything.

Such a child, while sitting in front of an interviewer, may climb on the back of the chair, over on the desk, hang his head down to the floor, or start hopping around the room like a wound-up puppet. It is important to note that some children have the capacity to control this inner-drivenness for a limited time, especially in a one-to-one interview or learning situation. This will not only allow them to learn under such circumstances but may also mislead the interviewer into doubting the excessive activity so clearly observed by the teacher at a time when the child is exposed to the classroom situation and is expected to sit still for longer periods without direct individual attention.

Hyperkinesis must be differentiated from the *overactivity* of the curious child who explores the new environment and moves from one area or object to the next as soon as he has discovered enough to satisfy him temporarily. Anxiety, too, can create over-activity, but this behavior is accompanied by other signs of anxiety such as fearfulness, noticeable in facial expression, re-luctance to enter a room or participate in a new activity, or associate with unfamiliar adults or children. Overactivity can also be observed in children who have never been accustomed to participating in an organized activity, either in their own home or in nursery schools or day care centers. The background history and evaluation of the home environment will help to identify such a child.

In the hyperkinetic child, the disappointment and disapproval of adults are readily conveyed to the child by the irritability of

the mother, her critical reaction, the stern disciplinary measures
of the father, or the avoidance of the tense situation by his
absence. Similar reactions may be experienced from babysitters and finally may lead to removal from the group, isolation
in nursery school, and exclusion from parties in neighbors' homes.
Similar disapproval and absence of recognition and rewards are
experienced in kindergarten and early grades.

Peer reactions are likely to be no less destructive. Children
are apt to avoid the disruptive element and resent the attention
the teacher is forced to give to this child. Fellow students may
ridicule him for his behavior and lack of ability "to do anything
right." Classmates soon learn what to expect of Charlie—that
his antics and the teacher's reaction can provide entertainment
and avoidance of learning tasks. If one day Charlie does not
perform as usual, the others will soon make it known to him
what they expect, thus frustrating any attempts on his part to
improve. The child's self-esteem is badly damaged. "I can
never do right, gain approval, be recognized in a positive way."

Since learning cannot take place under these circumstances,
no positive reinforcement can come from work well done. Avoidance as a defense reaction then serves to conceal failure: "I
didn't even try." "Not trying" is used by the child to avoid
criticism for not knowing. Blaming teachers and parents and
successful children for his failures projects the guilt upon others
and leads to the hostility so often observed in these children
and expressed in aggressive, destructive, and defiant behavior.
Aggressive behavior always brings attention, even though the
kind of attention given is critical or punitive. Aggressiveness
can also be ego supporting if the handicapped child can show
his physical superiority by hurting a weaker, academically
successful child.

Early detection of the causative relationship and appropriate
measures for prevention of subsequent problems can avoid many
of the harmful effects on the child's development. Behavior
caused by the interaction of organically and psychologically
determined factors and the reactions to and by persons in the
environment may become a way of life. Attempts to correct

such inappropriate behavior patterns once they become "fixed" may require massive and simultaneous educational, medical, and psychologic intervention which may be costly and time-consuming. Such a multidisciplinary approach is needed since the disturbance is now due to multifactorial causes.

The following diagram serves to describe graphically the interaction of the factors involved (Glaser, 1967).

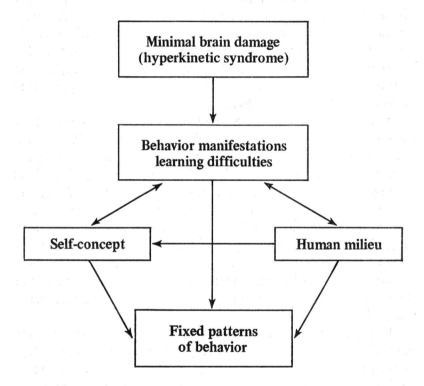

The use of special educational techniques which will reduce extraneous stimuli is one educational approach which has shown success. It would vary from the current standard classroom setting which usually has three groups of children doing different things at the same time, with stimulating material exposed on the classroom walls. For the hyperkinetic child, it has been found that individual instruction in small cubicles designed to reduce visual and auditory stimuli brings some success. Modern approaches, such as the "open-space school," offer so much distraction that they may have the opposite effect. Longer observations with these new educational techniques will be necessary to determine whether and how the special child can be integrated.

Some success has been obtained with medication. Here, too, controversy exists. Stimulants such as amphetamines and methylphenidate (Ritalin®) often have a calming effect on the hyperkinetic child. Imipramine, an antidepressant, and recently plain, strong coffee have been suggested (Schnackenberg, 1973). Since some of these medications are abused in today's drug culture, they have unfortunately and unjustifiably gone into disrepute for their legitimate and effective use.

A conference on the use of stimulant drugs, sponsored by the Office of Child Development, Department of Health, Education, and Welfare, in 1971, issued the following statement on the various treatment programs: ". . . Without specialized medical therapy, the consequences for these children of their failure to manage . . . even in an optimal environment . . . are clearly very severe. In such cases the aim is not to solve problems with drugs, but to put the severely handicapped child in a position to interact with his environment to the extent that his condition permits." . . . "Medicine does not 'cure' the condition, but the child may become more accessible to educational and counseling efforts."

Tranquilizers also have their place in reducing the anxiety in children who experienced failure, frustration, and humiliation by their peers. Here again public opinion is frequently hampering medical treatment. Parents wonder whether their children are being doped in order to make them less disturbing to the teacher rather than to make them more amenable to learning. The drowsiness produced by most of these medications at the onset of treatment gives support to this prejudice. The initial use of small doses and appropriate anticipatory explanations to child and parents can help overcome the opposition to the use of drugs and even enhance the placebo-effect of the medication.

Psychotherapy for the child may also be necessary at this stage but "individual psychotherapy per se is not adequate to treat hyperkinetic children unless the other necessary treatments are employed at the same time." (O'Malley and Eisenberg, 1973). Simultaneous counseling for the parents and consultations with teachers are generally indicated. In addition, parents and teachers of the hyperkinetic child are in need of occasional relief. However, parents often find it difficult to obtain babysitters, and teachers find it almost unbearable to cope with several hyperkinetic children in a large classroom. Smaller class size, especially designed classrooms, as well as specially trained teachers and teacher aides, can help most hyperkinetic children function in a group and benefit from the learning process. However, additional facilities should be available for separating the child from his regular classroom, not for punitive but for constructive purposes. If such a child has been overstimulated and is unable to function in his regular classroom, he should be separated from the group and taught for a measured period of time by a special teacher experienced in dealing with crisis situations. This will not only allow continuation of the educational process and calming of the child's behavior but should also have a reeducational emotional effect. Not only has he failed to avoid instruction through his behavior, but on the contrary he finds the learning process intensified and hopefully tolerable in a one-to-one approach.

Concurrent speech defects can seriously interfere with interpersonal relationships, and speech and language therapy is often indicated before school age. Poor handwriting, a frequent concomitant of minimal brain dysfunction, can evoke criticism and absorb much energy which the child could spend more profitably on content rather than form. The early use of the typewriter may greatly relieve the child's tension, while emphasis on improved penmanship—"if he really tries he can do it"—may only serve to increase his frustration. The child who really tries with maximum effort to produce legible and acceptable handwriting often does so at great sacrifice. Most of his energies are channeled into the efforts of producing good handwriting and reducing hyperactivity, with little energy left for concentrating on content of material which must be written down or on material presented by the teacher which must be understood and memorized.

GENETIC FACTORS AND SPECIFIC
READING DISABILITY

The acquisition of language skills, particularly reading, is a prerequisite for academic progress. Children who encounter persistent difficulties in learning to read are high-risk candidates for problems in academic achievement and school adjustment (Glaser and Clemmens, 1965). Dyslexia, congenital word blindness, specific developmental dyslexia, and strephosymbolia are terms used for those slow learners who have particular difficulty in learning the interpretation of symbols.

Rabinovitch (1962) uses the term "primary reading retardation" for this group, "brain injury with reading retardation" for those with "frank brain damage manifested by clearcut neurological deficits" and "secondary reading retardation" for all those children whose reading dysfunction is the result of psychiatric, educational, or other external influences.

There are professionals who do not believe that specific reading disability is an entity. They attribute the deficiency in the acquisition of reading skills to faulty teaching methods or to social, cultural, or emotional factors. They base their argument in part on the fact that retarded readers constitute a continuum from children with superior to average and below average reading ability and not a clearly circumscribed pathological entity.

Many professionals, however, believe that there exists an identifiable group of children with language and reading dysfunction who are of "normal" intellect, have been competently taught, and have no manifest physical or emotional problems. Their reading achievement is below their achievement in other school subjects. In later years, however, learning is affected in all subjects since reading, the basic tool for learning, has not been mastered. There is frequently a positive family history among the male ascendants. Boys are much more commonly affected than girls, and often minor neurological variants can be elicited in detailed and expanded neurological examinations. These consist of mixed laterality, delayed determination of handedness and awkwardness, specifically in fine motor coordination.

These neurological findings are often associated with some of the symptoms described under minimal brain dysfunction and thus make differentiation between this condition and Specific Reading Dysfunction almost impossible. This overlapping in symptomatology lends support to those who disclaim the existence of an entity of Specific Reading Disability. While demonstrable neurological findings and a history of traumatic or noxious assaults to the brain point in the direction of brain damage, reading difficulties present in other family members and the absence of evidence of neurological dysfunction suggest Specific Reading Disability. Only in a relatively small number of children can we state with certainty that their learning difficulty falls into one or the other category. (See diagram.)

Many other signs and symptoms occur in both conditions. The handwriting is usually poor and only maximal effort and concentration produce a form of handwriting acceptable to standard school requirements. There is disparity between the verbal and performance parts of psychometric tests such as the Wechsler Intelligence Scale for Children. Problems in spatial orientation and directionality as well as in visuomotor coordination can be demonstrated by the reproduction of designs as, for instance, in the Bender Gestalt test. Speech and language problems are commonly present. Hyperkinesis is believed to have organic origin in the brain damaged child ("inner-drivenness"), while the child with specific reading disability may be overactive (restless) due to anxiety.

Personal observations in private practice as well as experience in the Central Evaluation Clinic for Children of the University of Maryland have impressed this author with the high incidence of reading and language difficulties in brothers, fathers, and uncles of the children studied. It can be argued that there may be factors other than heredity contributing to the high incidence

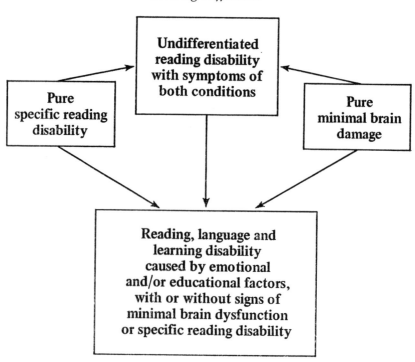

reported in males. Such factors may be greater emphasis on academic achievement in boys, maturational lag, and nature of resulting behavior manifestations. (Boys tend to act out, thus disturbing the teaching process, while girls are apt to be more withdrawn and are more likely overlooked or at least not referred for outside help.) The difference in the reported incidence, however, seems too great to be attributable only to these secondary factors.

Studies reported in the literature lend further support to genetic etiological factors. An exhaustive epidemiologic study of reading disabilities has been published by Hallgren (1960). He studied 276 cases of reading disability and their near relatives, as well as 212 controls. He found reading disabilities in 88 percent of the families of his index cases and concluded that reading problems are genetically determined and follow a dominant mode of inheritance.

Valuable information in understanding the contributing role

of hereditary and environmental factors may be gleaned from studies of twins with reading problems. Hermann (1958) reported studies on forty-five sets of twins in which at least one was found to have a reading problem. Of three pairs of nonidentical twins, one of whom had reading retardation, 33 percent of the co-twins were similarly involved. Of twelve sets of identical twins, however, 100 percent concordance was found. Although the numbers are small, the findings are of considerable interest and lend support to the hypothesis that genetic factors may be involved (Glaser and Clemmens, 1965).

An awareness of the possible influence of genetic factors is of more than academic interest. The presence of reading and learning difficulties in siblings or members of the parent generation could alert the educator or the pediatrician to the possible existence of such a handicap in a child who may show minimal signs of maladjustment in earliest school or preschool experiences. Early identification followed by special instructional approaches by teachers trained in corrective reading methods, together with psychological support for the child and counseling and guidance for teachers and parents can avoid or reduce the long term frustration, emotional consequences and academic failure experienced by undiagnosed children often inappropriately labeled as obstreperous, lazy, ill-behaved, or mentally retarded.

Educators and researchers are now looking into the possibility of objective identification of children with learning difficulties as early as three years of age. Legislation in Illinois recognizes children above three years of age with learning disabilities as eligible for special services in the public schools. Research is now in progress to design and validate a predictive battery of tests for the identification of prekindergarten children with potential learning problems. Project DIAL (Developmental Indicators for the Assessment of Learning) (1972) is now under way with the aim of developing screening tests and recommendations for the "intervention, amelioration, preventive and/or remedial programs for prekindergarten children with potential learning problems." The authors have reviewed the available screening and testing material for small children in a most comprehensive study.

It has been suggested that dyslexia does not exist among people whose language is phonetic, that is, where each sound is represented by a symbol—very unlike the English language, where pronunciation and spelling often do not show such a direct relationship and spelling must often be learned by rote. George Bernard Shaw cited as example of the illogic of English spelling the word "fish" which, he stated, could be spelled "ghoti"—taking the sounds from enou*gh*, w*o*men, and na*ti*on. Inconsistencies like these certainly present difficulties in integrating spoken and written language. Hermann (1959) wrote that "the greater the divergence between pronunciation and written language, the more difficult it will be for the word-blind (and for that matter the normal child) to acquire the art of reading and writing."

It has been claimed that dyslexia does not exist in Spanish speaking countries. Money (1962) did not believe this, stating that "phonetic regularity is of no help to a child who cannot remember the name and sound of each letter." Money also quotes two Japanese neuropsychiatrists, Kuromaru and Okada, who reported the case of a Japanese boy who had difficulties with the syllabary, phonetic system of writing in Japanese, which resembles our alphabetic system, while he had less difficulty with the ideographic system (symbols for entire words or concepts). Although this system is harder to learn originally, the recognition of the meaning of the ideograph is easier for the child who has difficulties in breaking up words into sounds and letters.

While "some variations based on the particular languages to be learned and the manner of their teaching . . ." can be expected, ". . . the basic problem is world-wide, apparently part of 'the human condition' . . ." (Matejcek, 1971). "It's the same the whole world over . . ." was the subtitle of a Symposium on Dyslexia International (McLeod, 1972), with the world literature reporting dyslexia in many countries (Czechoslovakia, Japan, China, Sweden, Denmark).

There is no reason to assume, therefore, that developmental dyslexia occurs only in certain nations, races, or languages. A statistical appraisal of its relative incidence is impossible at this time because of the difference in the character of the language, the methods of teaching, and also because of a considerable amount of underreporting or misdiagnosis. Even within the same school system children who cannot read may simply be labeled retarded while others may be called dyslexic, no matter what the nature of their disability may be. Not being able to read can also have the connotation of being stupid or lazy, or of poor teaching, and one can assume hesitation in reporting by teachers and parents as a defensive maneuver. However, the lack of accurate statistical reporting should not prevent us from early and vigorous institution of remedial methods in those children in whom the condition is recognized.

CHAPTER II

INTELLIGENCE AND LEARNING DIFFICULTIES

$\mathbf{M}$ENTAL FUNCTIONING AND, with it, learning ability are strongly correlated with intellectual ability. Kanner (1972) lists among "the cognitive or intellectual functions . . . comprehension, thinking, reasoning, judgment, inventiveness, skills, information, and utilization of past experiences."

ASSESSMENT OF INTELLIGENCE

Measurements to establish the intellectual level are obtained through various tests designed to establish an intelligence quotient, a numerical expression of the child's intellectual functioning in relation to his peers.

The level of functioning is influenced by innate ability or "natural endowment" (Rapaport, 1945), past experience, attitude toward the testing situation and the tester, and emotional and physical health. While we assume at present that innate ability is a fixed congenital factor, the other components are variable and subject to external influences. Thus I.Q. test results can be expected to vary somewhat in the same individual at different times.

Since the days of the early pioneers in the field (Binet, Goddard, Terman, between 1905 and 1920) new tests have been designed, revised, and adapted to meet the characteristics of different cultures. They were intended to identify the mentally defective or the gifted, or generally to establish the child's level of functioning.

As with any laboratory test, I.Q. test results must be viewed with caution and in the proper perspective. I.Q. tests in this country were standardized on the "average" American with an average environmental and educational background. While the purpose may be to measure intellectual endowment, they actually reflect the individual's current functioning, and in this capacity they fill a vital need.

Implied in the data of an I.Q. is its predictive value and, understandably, this has led to controversy. Theoretically only that part of the test result which reflects innate endowment would be stable and unchanging, while any experiential components would be subject to change. Thus a test standardized on averages of a certain population should be expected to be valid only on similar population samples. However, its value as a measurement for the intellectual endowment of an individual whose experiential and attitudinal background is never "average" is being questioned. Although attempts at designing so-called culture-free or culture-fair tests have been numerous, they have never been and probably never can be totally satisfactory. Anastasi (1968) stated that "no one test can be universally applicable or equally 'fair' to all cultures."

A child who has not had "average" intellectual stimulation and has not been exposed to learning experiences usually expected in his age group is apt to function below the highly stimulated child who has been exposed intensively to learning materials. Thus test results can be misleading as to actual intellectual ability and future potential.

Extensive work on the subject has been done by Rosenberg (1968) at the Johns Hopkins University School of Medicine. He designed the Johns Hopkins Perceptual Test to identify the bright among children in the low socioeconomic status population. He contends that poor school performance may be due to the school's failure to teach the child rather than the child's low learning ability. Although the results of his study seem promising, the author himself indicates the need for further investigation to validate his findings.

It is the task of the skilled, experienced tester to recognize the child whose performance on the test is depressed as a result of extraneous difficulties such as fatigue, fear, antagonism, or sensory handicaps. Repetition of the test at a different time, alleviation of fear and antagonism through preparatory interviews, or correction of the visual or hearing handicap would then allow the child to perform on a higher level. It can be a very difficult task to recognize the child whose innate ability is relatively high but whose functioning and performance on tests is reduced by lack of experience, environmental deprivation, faulty or insufficient schooling, or severe psychological traumata (Glaser and Eisenberg, 1956).

Performance on standardized tests is also influenced by cultural factors. The child may have learned many skills which tests do not examine and which may not be considered useful or desirable in the general society but may be important or even necessary for survival in the subculture of the child's family. This dilemma is of some practical significance, for it may be assumed that the child whose performance on a test and in school is below his innate ability due to past environmental factors, could catch up if properly taught and stimulated. He should then be able to enter the mainstream of school children and later of adult society.

Thus far the successes in this endeavor have not been very great. The reasons for this are still subject to speculation; perhaps we have not found the proper educational techniques, or we have not been able to make sufficient changes in the ongoing environmental influences, or it may be that previous attitudinal influences and deprivations simply cannot be overcome once the optimal developmental period is past.

Some attempts in recent years have focused on the prevention of deprivation by entering children into a stimulating environment prior to the customary school age (Program Head Start and others). In children between the ages of three to five improvements in functioning on various tests were observed immediately following the exposure to the intensified programs. However, these children seemed to lose their relative gains after several years in a regular classroom. These findings indicate the need for a continuing special program beyond the level usually offered in public schools to children in deprived sub-cultural areas (McDill, 1969; White, 1970).

It was further speculated that earlier intensified stimulation (birth to three years) may be even more effective in preserving the endowed capacities of the child, and day care centers were proposed to accomplish this aim. These day centers would not only offer a stimulating environment for the child during several hours of the day but may also allow the mother to enter employment and attain a more satisfying independent and self-respecting existence. Her improved self-concept plus supervised observation or courses on child rearing techniques may further enhance her effectiveness as a mother.

Rosenberg (1973) described the experiences with a group of four-year-old children and their parents at the Martin Luther King, Jr. Center for Parents and Children, attached to Johns Hopkins University School of Medicine. He demonstrated the beneficial effect upon the motivation and performance of children exposed to the program and showed that the maintenance of these achievements was strongly influenced by the behavior of the adults significant in the child's world. It should be pointed out that program Head Start has always included strong parent participation and education components in its child education and health programs.

The significance of the intellectual ability of a particular child and his family with regard to their chances for adapting adequately to the demands of society will depend upon the cultural, intellectual, and economic level of society and cannot be judged in isolation.

MILD MENTAL RETARDATION

The obvious difficulties experienced by a child with moderate or severe mental retardation are not the subject of this discussion. However, mild mental retardation is often not recognized in the preschool child. While in itself it may need no special intervention at that stage, it can be the cause of parental frustration and disappointment with the slow developmental process. This in turn can produce in the child feelings of frustration, inability to please the parents or compete with siblings, and a tendency to avoid "learning" in order to conceal his inability and avoid failure.

Kanner (1972) suggests the term "intellectual inadequacy" rather than deficiency, indicating that these individuals are inadequate to function in our intellectually oriented society. They may be quite adequate in a primitive culture or in simpler, mechanical occupations in our current society.

Since our schools are geared toward education for intellectually more demanding careers, these children fail and their inadequacy is made apparent. Perhaps a radically revised curriculum which would prepare them for realistically attainable occupational goals would reduce frustrations and embarrassments and allow them to develop into emotionally healthier adults who are prepared for and satisfied with the jobs which they can perform well.

An accurate early evaluation, based on a reliable and objective developmental assessment and appropriate psychological tests, is necessary to allow for interpretation and guidance for the parents. Placement in a specially qualified nursery school (not necessarily a special school for the mentally retarded) should condition and prepare the child for school.

The possible coexistence of dyslexia and mild mental retardation must be considered. If reading achievement is below the expected level in relation to the mental rather than the chronological age of the child, dyslexia can be suspected. Such children may be helped through special instructional techniques in reading to reach *their* potential. It is important that parents and teachers keep in mind that the optimal reading level the given retarded child will reach will be below the average of the general population. Overenthusiasm on the part of adults can lead to frustration and disappointment which may cause greater damage than the reading disability itself.

RELATIVE RETARDATION

A discrepancy in intellectual levels between one child and the rest of his family might be cause for trouble. For instance, a child of average intellect born into a family of above average ability may be considered retarded *relative* to his environment. Through assortative mating and migration we usually find both parents of higher intellectual, educational, and economic standards, and living in a community of families of similar endowment. The child of "only" average intelligence will show slower speech development and learning responses than his brighter siblings and neighbors. His comprehension will be slower than that of his peers, beginning in nursery school and continuing throughout the school years. The bright parents with high educational expectations and aspirations will be anxious about his "slowness." When they turn to professionals they may be "reassured" that the child is of average (i.e. normal) intelligence. To them this signifies that he is capable of performing like their other children and his peers. They tend to overlook the fact that they live in an enclave of brighter than average children and adults. Parents and teachers then are disappointed and annoyed by his "laziness." A misguided effort may be made to push the child beyond his capacity.

D.T.'s mother called for an appointment because her fourteen-year-old daughter had always been a behavior problem, was not doing well academically, and going down further during the last months. In the initial contact mother stated, "she can't accept our direction, nor can she discipline herself, maybe because she is the baby in the family." Mother continued: "She feels that she is less than her sisters." The older daughters were very good students. D. felt competition, gave up, and was unhappy.

D. described herself as the "stupid little sister and a disappointment to the parents." She had periods of depression during which she remained in her room and was noncommunicative with the parents. She showed hostility toward parents who "gave me everything and are so good to me." It was not until later in therapy that she was able to recognize that the parents did not give her "everything"—namely recognition and acceptance for the way she was and not for what the parents wanted her to be.

Her I.Q. was 106, she was physically attractive and engaged in many social activities. The family lived in a suburban area and the child attended a school where academic achievement was valued highly and the majority of children were college bound. Parents and child had to learn to accept that her ability, although "average," was not up to the intellectual level of her family and most of her peers and that she might not be able to go to college or at least not to the schools her sisters were attending.

The emotional consequences to such frustrating experiences for child, parents, and teachers can be devastating. Since the child is unable to understand or explain what is happening, usually ineffective and inappropriate defense reactions will appear. They may be various devices of avoidance, reaction formation, acting-out or attention-getting mechanisms. In severe cases this neurotic process can lead to a psychotic reaction (see Major Psychiatric Disorders).

It is not clear whether such a psychotic reaction, which has been observed in youngsters who have been followed through childhood and into young adulthood, is the result of the unusual stress to which they had been exposed, whether the child's cerebral condition had rendered him more vulnerable, or whether syndromes which are diagnosed in childhood as mild mental retardation, minimal brain dysfunction, learning disability, and in later life as schizophrenic psychosis are, in certain individuals, variations of the same basic pathological condition.

An early psycho-educational program is even more important if mild mental retardation or relative retardation is combined with the hyperkinetic syndrome, specific learning disability, or with emotional problems. It seems that a significant number of children with minimal brain dysfunction fall into this category. Their intelligence quotient may be below the average of the general population or they may be members of bright families and their I.Q. may range ten to thirty points below those measured or estimated in parents and siblings. Thus a double problem exists: learning disability and/or minimal brain dysfunction on one hand, and subaverage intellectual functioning on the other. If the relative reduction in I.Q. scores in such a child is the result of the same noxious influence which caused the minimal brain dysfunction, thus is organically determined, it is presumably not remediable. If the lowered I.Q. scores are, however, the result of educational deprivation secondary to minimal brain dysfunction or their psychological sequels, they may possibly be preventable or corrigible.

E.D.'s father stated: "I was told the boy had average intelligence, so he should be able to do what every other boy does. E. can do anything he wants to do. I was fat and could do no sports, but I set my mind to it and learned."

The boy, age thirteen, with an I.Q. of ninety-four, had mild cerebral palsy, spoke and wrote with difficulty, and was excused from physical education. While he was able to perform with help at a passing level in the lower grades, his increasing difficulties were the result of his physical handicap in the presence of only average intellect.

The dual nature of the handicap was not recognized or accepted by the father, and the boy was unable to comply with his father's wishes for better performance. He became dejected and developed symptoms of compulsion and phobias.

In order to help these children succeed in school and prevent the development of psycho-educational complications, a realistic appraisal of the child's abilities and handicaps in all areas is needed. On the basis of these findings an educational and vocational course must be charted to reach a *realistic* goal. The child, his parents, and the educators must be counseled to help them understand and accept such plans and actions.

RELATIVE INTELLECTUAL SUPERIORITY

Another situation which may interfere with the learning process occurs when an unusually bright child is born into a family of average or below average intellectual endowment or low educational achievement. Such a child may be frustrated from his earliest years by not having his inquisitive mind satisfied or stimulated. Through assortative migration the parents are apt to live among people of similar level of functioning, and the school population is likely to reflect the parental level of intellectual achievement and motivation.

Such a superior child will show boredom in a school which is geared to an average or even below average intellectual and educational level and which may not satisfy his curiosity and his intellectual needs by a flexible, stimulating curriculum. He will look for other activities in the classroom, become disinterested in the teaching process, and disturb others. He may not only present a behavior problem but may actually fail in his school work since he was mentally not present when the material was discussed. Unless the physician specifically inquires about academic and behavioral school adjustment or the educator recognizes this discrepancy during the earliest school experiences, serious damage may be done to the psychological and educational development of the child.

But it is not only the bright child born into a not-so-bright family who is hampered in his development. We have generally failed to provide effective school settings for the gifted child to help him experience inner comfort, which is an essential ingredient of proficiency. Kanner (1971) suggests that "society must find new devices for helping gifted people make natural use of their ability."

Newman *et al.* (1973) studied the behavior of fifteen gifted boys with I.Q.'s over 130 who underachieved. They pointed out that high I.Q. scores may reflect only some parts of a superior development. High verbal skills, often expressed also in superior reading ability, do not guarantee overall superior functioning and may actually produce conflicts which may interfere with the development of affective maturation and physical skills.

Parental attitudes of overemphasizing and rewarding verbal skills may cause the child to invest all efforts into gaining acceptance and admiration from adults by overdeveloping the use of words, often even without deeper thought and understanding. The authors point out the psychodynamic complications in these children and especially the difficulties of finding an integrated school program for them: "Current concepts of 'ungraded education' frequently offer the best solution for such children." Such a program should ". . . help to develop all functions, the 'bright functions,' the 'deficit functions,' and the often obscure 'average functions.' "

In any child with above average intellectual ability whose school performance is below expectation the possibility of dyslexia must be considered. Being superior in many functions, the bright child may be able to cover up his disability for some time and may even be able to compensate for the defect. Recognition and assistance could thus be delayed. On the other hand, he could show an emotional reaction to the unrecognized disability which may so overshadow the learning disability that psychotherapy may be suggested while overlooking the need for reading remediation.

CHAPTER III

ENVIRONMENTAL FACTORS

THE HOME INFLUENCE

THE NATURE AND significance of parental influences upon the psychosocial-educational development of the *handicapped* child has been discussed in connection with the respective handicap. Parental influences which may lead to *inner conflicts* interfering with learning will be discussed in Chapter IV, "Psychological Factors." This chapter deals with the characteristics of the home environment which may have a direct effect on the healthy child's learning process. Recognition of these characteristics can give the professional a clue to the reason for educational malfunctioning and point the way to its correction.

Family Mobility

Mobility of the family is one of the phenomena of our culture on all economic levels. Each year a significant number of children are dislodged from their familiar surroundings. They lose their friends and change their schools. There are differences in standards and curriculum between different school systems, even between different schools in the same system.

This presents a problem of academic continuity and readiness even for the good student. When the move is made during the school year rather than during summer vacation, the discontinuity is even greater. The "new child" is often not accepted socially and, if he is ahead of the students in the new class, may be viewed as "smart alec" and "show off" or, if he has not covered the subject under study, as "dummy." Such an introduction can be destructive to his self-esteem and may lead to neurotic adaptive behavior (not volunteering, not answering for fear of ridicule, or psychosomatic complaints to avoid school, or simply refusal to go to school). Parental support may be lacking during these critical times since both parents are under the strain of the move, even if such move is by choice and designed to lead to the improvement of living standards. Often the bread winner moves ahead of the family, leaving the mother with increased responsibility before and after the move.

Timing and strategy of the family move can often be influenced by professional guidance to the benefit of the children involved. Achievement tests can help in proper class or group placement or point out the need for individual tutoring. Counseling may help with early adjustment difficulties. This might preferably be done by school counselors, who can deal with the problems as they arise and in their proper perspective. The use of outside agencies or private sources usually is not as effective in this kind of situation as delay is inevitable and the focus is apt to be on more diffuse issues rather than on the specific difficulty presenting itself in school.

Competitiveness

Competitiveness affects all phases of our lives. Parents may push their children beyond their capacity in a conscious or subconscious effort to "keep up with the Jones's." This competitiveness at times takes on epidemic forms in individual schools or neighborhoods. Children are driven to compulsive preoccupation with learning, or they acquire undesirable personality traits such as cheating or harming a successful child's progress to advance their own standing. They may also develop neurotic symptoms or total negativism toward school.

K.I.'s father was the only one of three boys who had not attended college, and he felt that he did not want his son to miss this opportunity. The twelve-year-old boy, with an I.Q. of 100, expressed his feelings about his father by saying, "My father wanted to be something better than a car mechanic. . . . I don't want to follow what father wants me to do . . . failing will get me out of school earlier. . . . I want to be a hobo."

H.S. was the son of an ambitious businessman whose own work schedule did not differentiate between day and night. He had the greatest aspirations for his boy whom he described as "not an ordinary boy." He was referred to the author at fifteen years of age because of sleep difficulties and various physical complaints (psychosomatic) which kept him out of school. He was taking an accelerated program, studied the violin, participated in two orchestras and other extra-curricular activities. He had to be "tops" in all he did, including all school subjects.

He had indicated to his parents for the longest time that he wanted to stop violin lessons: "Why prepare for a career which I don't want." But the family was "proud to have a violinist." The preceding spring he was to have gone to an audition. He was staggering as he entered the father's car to ride there, and mother suggested that he not go. During the ride H. became progressively more silent and when they arrived at the music school he was unconscious and cyanotic. He was rushed to a hospital where it was found that he had taken an overdose of sleeping pills. He stated later: "I had to *show* my father that I really did not want music. He did not listen to me when I told him."

H. continued to show signs of depression and suicidal tendencies for which he was later hospitalized for several months.

This boy's competitive spirit and his need to be the best in all of his enterprises, which had been forced upon him by his father's ambition, had led to his emotional collapse. Warning symptoms had been noticeable in his behavior and attitude at school as well as at home. If they had been heeded earlier, the severe mental condition which followed could probably have been prevented.

Low Motivation

Environmental influences may be the cause of low motivation to learn. In contrast to the competitiveness in certain circles as mentioned in the preceding paragraphs, parental indifference toward education may counteract any incentive the child may have on his own.

Blue collar families, with a limited educational background, may see little value in the refinements of education which they themselves had missed. They may be unable to comprehend the changing demands of our mechanized, automated society and may see their children's future only in terms of their own achievements. The child, on his part, may accept the parents' outlook on life.

K.C., a fourteen-year-old boy, was referred because of failure in all subjects and lack of motivation. K. was very close to his father who had been employed for many years by the same firm as forklift operator. The father was proud of his steady work record and accepting of his position in life. When the father took chronically ill, the son could see no other career but to operate father's forklift. He, like his father, saw no reason to advance his education beyond the very basic skills of elementary school. When the child was asked what he would do if the machinery needed maintenance or repair work, his reply was that he would call the mechanic; he saw no need to read a manual or understand the mechanism. What if a new model would be introduced, would he not have to read the instructions? No, the foreman would teach him.

There are, of course, many youngsters in blue collar families who, having been exposed from early childhood to many levels of occupation, income, and standards of living through the mass media, may not be satisfied with the life style of their parents. "In our modern society it seems it should not be necessary to inform families about the value of education. However, such is the case often. To change a child's set of values without changing the family's attitudes is like trying to make him disloyal to his own family. Most all of us would resist such manipulations." (Simmons, 1959).

When the young man realizes that his dreams for higher achievements would have required a better early educational background, he may become disillusioned and angry. He will then project his anger at society, which does not "offer" him the opportunity for advancement (for which he is not prepared) or at his parents who "didn't make me go to school and learn." It is the unusual adolescent or young adult who then has the self-control and the opportunity to give up the chance for immediate income, even though limited, for schooling now and higher income later. Having to study elementary school material at a later age also hurts his self-concept and is difficult to admit to his peers without loss of status.

Certainly uneducated parents do not always have such a stymying influence upon their children's learning. There are many individuals with high educational achievements in the midst of poverty, illiteracy, and failure. Entire cultural or ethnic subgroups have placed their emphasis on the education of their children and have shown that within one generation phenomenal changes in educational standards can occur. Program Head Start has attempted for several years to educate parents of preschool children in the hope that they will sustain the child's progress made during his Head Start experience and encourage and seek such progress in their other children.

Low motivation is not limited to low socioeconomic groups. While the mode of living in middle and upper classes usually offers motivation and stimulus for learning, the reverse may also be true.

C.I., a junior high school girl, was performing considerably below her ability. The parents, on a conscious intellectual level, were demanding good school performance. Mother was not working but was engaged in various volunteer and recreational activities.

In counseling sessions mother was able to look at her real feelings about working women. She stated that for a woman holding a job was a sign of failure in marriage. It meant that she had failed to find a man who could provide her with all the necessities and luxuries which she considered signs of happiness. Learning and training for gainful employment was thus considered preparation for failure in marriage. This even applied to the learning of domestic skills which "should be performed by a maid."

After the mother gained insight, she and the therapist were able to help her daughter reappraise the current and past history of the family. It emerged that during the earlier years of marriage mother not only did all the housework herself but also held a job to increase the family income. She was even able to admit that these years of mutual struggle were some of her happiest. Her daughter's outlook toward school and life in general changed after mother had gained an understanding of her own feelings and was able to communicate them to her daughter.

Economic Factors

Economic factors may interfere with a child's school attendance. A lack of shoes or clothing keeps some children of poor families, especially in rural America, from attending school. The need to increase family income influences some sixteen-year-olds to leave school and seek employment. The absent parent (working mother, absent father) may cause the child to be late for school, forget school supplies, be unsupervised in his homework, or go to school inadequately dressed or fed.

Parental Neglect

Neglectful parents on all economic and educational levels can have detrimental effects upon their children similar to those caused by poverty and ignorance. The child who does not perform and appears fatigued or is hungry may come from a well-to-do home with a mother who is not willing to get up in the morning and send the child off to school in an orderly and well prepared fashion. The father may leave for work earlier or may even be home but unwilling to take on "mother's duties."

While parental counseling may be helpful in such situations, lifelong habits are not easily changed. At times drastic intervention by social or legal agencies is necessary to break the pattern of academic underachievement due to parental neglect. Unfortunately neither social, legal nor economic approaches have been very successful in changing the life styles of major segments of our population.

Distracting Factors

Distracting factors play a role in some cases of school failure. Television and audio equipment in the child's room are temptations and distractions competing with books for the child's attention. While this is a phenomenon in the middle and upper class family, crowded living conditions in poorer families deprive the child of the privacy and quiet he needs for study.

Counseling can influence some families to structure study and recreational resources in the house so as to minimize competition. The public library occasionally can help to provide the quiet atmosphere conducive to studying even in the family with crowded living space and many small children.

Deprivation

"The term 'cultural deprivation' refers to the situation in which the child's opportunity to utilize fully his intellectual potentials or to achieve scholastically is impaired because of limited environmental experiences, constricted language development and minimal valuation of intellectual or academic activities." (Friedman, 1962).

Negative parental attitudes toward learning can cause lack ,f motivation. Books, magazines, and newspapers are not readily available and active stimulation and participation by the parents in school-related activities is absent. Pleasurable learning experiences such as trips to the library or museum exhibits are limited. The parents' own language ability is low and verbal intercourse is constricted. Intellectual and academic activities, if any, are passive and minimal. While this does not necessarily hold to all low socioeconomic minority groups, it is found there much more frequently (Jones, 1954).

In any therapeutic approach it must be kept in mind that many of the above mentioned factors are essentially social problems which must be attacked by "feeding the hungry, educating the ignorant, treating the emotionally disturbed"—in that order (Simmons, 1959). Economic assistance, retraining of the breadwinner, relocation of the family may be the basic steps. In addition, early educational experiences to counteract the effects of deprivation have been attempted through the establishment of nursery school classes in public school systems in underprivileged areas (Glaser and Clemmens, 1965).

Adaptation of the school curriculum to meet the special needs of children in such areas is another way to increase their motivation to learn and remain in school. This should not mean a deprived curriculum for the deprived child, but a meaningful curriculum geared to the practical need for early tangible returns: early introduction of vocational skills, with academic teaching as a meaningful adjunct to vocational training rather than emphasis placed on academic subjects which are of little practical value to the youngster who must look for early gainful employment.

CULTURAL INFLUENCE

Social Pressure

Social pressure by a peer group unmotivated toward educational goals and antagonistic toward authority figures who represent the established society, such as teachers, will have a continuing negative effect upon school performance in any child striving for peer recognition. This phenomenon is well known among low socioeconomic groups and among minority groups who, although envious of the educated person's successes, project upon him the role of oppressor. While a few will "identify with the aggressor" and strive to emulate him to reach or exceed his level, the majority will find it easier to use escape and avoidance as defense and stop active participation in the educational process.

The need for immediate gratification of wants is normal for the very young but continues in the immature adolescent or even adult. The desire to start working and making money to buy a car or to gain independence from the parents may override the outlook for possible higher earnings after completion of further education. Since job opportunity and earning capacity are influenced also by factors other than the educational background—such as racial, ethnic, and religious prejudices, parental educational and occupational levels, and the job market—the young person is apt to use these factors as excuses for satisfying his immediate desires: "It won't make any difference anyway, so I may just as well stop school and make money now."

Psychological Impact of Cultural Factors

Economic factors, as described above, are often reinforced by their psychological impact. Cars and motorcycles are symbols of power and strength, manliness and independence. A weak ego and low self-esteem receive a boost by the power of the machine under the person's control. The machine therefore must be of high horsepower, great noise, and strong eye appeal, adorned with shiny and conspicuous gadgets and decorations to advertise the strength and success of its owner. The machine thus replaces the lacking educational or social or economic status of the individual.

This defensive maneuver is quite understandable and, to a certain degree, used universally. The individual lacking personal satisfaction of his narcissistic needs or experiencing an economic setback or other blow to his self-esteem often resorts to the purchase of visible items of embellishment (new clothes, hair styles) or economic symbols of success (new car, new house) to strengthen his lagging morale.

While such defensive reactions may help the individual over temporary mood swings or mild periods of depression, they do not provide the solution of the underlying conflict. This solution would have to come either through correction of the deficiency (return to education or training to achieve higher goals) or through acceptance of the status in life and the giving up of unattainable and therefore unrealistic goals. Such acceptance can take place only if the person can gain insight and understanding of his abilities, resources, psychological and economic needs as well as the impact of cultural influences. These cultural influences begin with the immediate family and extend to the subculture of one's community and ethnic or social subgroups and finally to the country and the world as a whole.

Psychiatric counseling may help some individuals to clarify their position and find a solution. However, psychiatric help is usually requested and obtainable only by middle and upper class youth in whom this type of conflict occurs infrequently.

Wandering Youth

The symptom of "wandering youth" is in part at least produced by youth's dissatisfaction with existing cultural phenomena and a search for other modes of living more suitable to their desires. The tremendous expansion of air and car travel has contributed to the growth of this phenomenon but it certainly has not been the cause of it.

The young person who has reached a certain level of maturity which enables him to recognize his needs and assess his environment may look for a different environment rather than adapt to one that is not conducive to his needs. This search and mobility, while not supportive of the systematic pursuit of a relatively rigid educational process, may constitute a learning experience of a different nature and lead to emotional maturation and balance.

Shift of Values

Some of youth's dissatisfaction seems to originate from a shift in values and the need to establish an independent identity. This may explain the lack of motivation for learning in some children of educated middle and upper class parents. Here the need to establish an independent identity is often expressed by the desire to be different from and opposite to the parental image. Educational preparation for jobs respected by the parental generation and leading to materially rewarding occupations is therefore rejected. Return to the "simple life" is given as a reason for shunning established educational careers.

Unfortunately the rewards of such a life style are usually not forthcoming since our technologically developed, materialistically oriented society offers little opportunity for success without educational background. The conflict between the desire for an idealistic life style and the comforts of material goods, between the ideals of youth and the pragmatic approach of the adult world is difficult for many young people to resolve or tolerate.

Rebellion Against Categorization

Another frequently challenged practice is the method of judging the individual's ability to perform a job or function on the basis of an elaborate system of *certification and classification*. While such a system is probably necessary in our complicated technological society, it forces the individual into a predetermined mold. The adolescent sees hypocrisy in the professed high esteem for individuality in this country and finds his desire for individuation and independence violated. He rebels against the system and the educational process which is geared toward preparing him to fit into a category and documents his fitness through certification. Since the system is fairly rigid, the adolescent who has dropped out of the educational process finds himself excluded from the opportunity to work in areas where he may feel to have capabilities. He is unable to accept or admit that he does not meet the formal experiential or educational requirements and resents that this regimentation does not fit into the idealistic picture of individuality and personal initiative.

These psycho-cultural conflicts may lead to learning difficulties such as performance below ability level or complete separation from school. This escape, however, is not sufficient to solve the conflict nor to help the individual cope with his difficulties in life adjustment.

Drug Abuse

In searching for further avenues of escape from this dilemma, some turn to drugs to gain a temporary feeling of relief and well being. This, of course, is only one factor leading to drug abuse, a condition which has assumed increasing importance within the educational field. Drug abuse in itself frequently causes school failure through a variety of influences such as association with nonmotivated youth, need to work or steal to support the habit, or chemical interference with intellectual activity.

While stimulants may temporarily increase working capacity, they ultimately lead to exhaustion and inability to retain learning material. Sedatives reduce mental alertness and, like mood alterators, give the feeling of tranquility and satisfaction on a chemical basis without achievement or growth. Hallucinogenic drugs, of course, transport the individual into a world of unreality and dream and leave him unprepared for the vicissitudes of the real world. When drug effects wear off and the world appears as cold and demanding as before the use of drugs, the desire to return to the satisfaction of the dream world is a powerful influence to continue the drug use. Ultimately a habit is established and the regular use of drugs becomes a way of life which is incompatible with concentrated educational efforts.

CHAPTER IV

PSYCHOLOGICAL FACTORS

SCHOOL PERSONNEL AND parents may be puzzled by a sudden arrest in academic progress or by behavior changes occurring without apparent reason in a child who in the past had been functioning well. Without recognizable warning signals, grades may begin to go down in a previously good student, and an outgoing, pleasant child may become withdrawn, moody, or frequently absent from school. It is in the interest of the child that such changes be recognized early, the cause established and remedial measures instituted because the experience of school difficulties affects the child's self-esteem as well as his relationship with peers, teachers, and parents.

Prolonged physical absence from school or mental absence from the learning process from whichever cause are psychologically traumatic in themselves. The task of catching up with missed learning material increases with each day of absence. Not knowing the study material and having to make up fictitious excuses for an absence are embarrassing and anxiety provoking and thus contribute further to learning difficulties.

STRESS UNRELATED TO THE LEARNING PROCESS

Psychological stress, regardless of the underlying dynamics or cause, consume energy and may result in insomnia, day dreaming, an inability to concentrate, and a lowering of learning capacity. It affects children of all ages and in all socioeconomic groups.

In the following a variety of psychological factors will be

presented which are apt to occur in school age children. Recognition of the existence of these conflicts may help solve the puzzle of a child's academic failure or behavior change.

Domestic Conflicts

K.D., a twelve and one-half-year-old intelligent boy who had had previous contact with this therapist, called for an appointment because he had "lots of trouble in school." He was attending private school and his grades had declined suddenly and sharply.

In the first interview he was able to talk about the acute severe marital crisis of his parents which threatened the foundation of the family unit. Fortunately the acute crisis was resolved rapidly, followed by immediate improvement of school performance. Needless to say, the deeper marital discord had existed for some years. The need for marriage counseling was now recognized by the parents, and the boy continued in therapy to help him cope with the difficult domestic situation.

It is rare that presenting symptoms can be alleviated so promptly because there is usually a delay in seeking professional help, while school difficulties persist and cause secondary psychological and educational problems.

Changes in Family Composition

Separation or threatened separation from parents through death, illness, or divorce commonly affects academic performance in the child.

The arrival of a new person in the household, such as a new baby or an old or sick dependent relative, or the presence of a chronically ill or handicapped sibling can also be stressful. The parents are increasingly preoccupied with the dependent person, and attitudinal changes may occur in the parents as a result of the influence exerted upon them by the new family member.

V.I., an impulsive child with explosive temper outbursts leading to physical violence, had finally gained sufficient self-control to limit his expression of anger to words. His school adjustment was marginal. Mother had learned to tolerate this verbal behavior, having a vivid memory of earlier acting out episodes.

When the maternal grandmother moved in with the family and voiced disapproval of the child's "disrespect" and verbal abuse, she put pressure on him as well as on his mother to correct this behavior. The ensuing constant pressure by both women led to renewed violence and running away episodes and decrease in school performance.

L.S., a four-year-old boy, was referred because of rebellious behavior which included misconduct at nursery school and reluctance of attendance. The father had tried to rear the child in military discipline. Although difficulties in management had existed before, they were not brought to professional attention until they were observed by school personnel. The young and inexperienced parents had used as a model the father's recollection of his own upbringing. The father also desired to please his own father, a former military man who lived nearby and visited frequently.

It was interesting to observe the change in father's attitude after he gained insight into the reasons for his approach to his child and recognized that it was contrary to his independent ideas of child rearing. When he was able to discuss the matter with his own father, he was relieved to learn that his strict disciplinarian father had considerably mellowed in his grandfatherly role. Once this conflict was resolved, the child responded well to an approach geared to his own rather than his father's needs.

Physical Conditions Leading to Psychological Stress

Precocious or delayed sexual development can cause emotional stress. Even if signs of puberty, such as menstruation, breast growth, appearance of pubic hair, size of genitalia, and change of voice, are adequately explained in anticipatory counseling with child and parents, the early or late manifestation of these signs will set such a child apart from others. This can become particularly worrisome when privacy is denied by compulsory showers following gym periods in junior high school (age twelve to fifteen). This forces disclosure and often is followed by teasing, ridicule, and embarrassment. The same applies to youngsters with physical defects or abnormalities which can be successfully hidden prior to nude exposure in school. The defect may be as minor as webtoes (two or more toes grown together) or as disturbing as gynecomastia (breast enlargement in boys). Unusual physical size may also present difficulties in peer and adult relationships and create stressful situations interfering with the learning process. The very small child often becomes the teacher's pet and conjures up the wrath of his classmates, while the very tall may face expectations according to size rather than chronological ability and maturity.

S.L., an extremely tall, handsome and bright twelve-year-old boy was promoted to the accelerated program of junior high school. He developed fears of school, vomiting and abdominal pains. It soon became apparent how troubled he was about his lack of opportunity to measure himself in physical competition. His classmates were too small, and sixteen or seventeen-year-old youngsters, while of his size or smaller, were much superior to him in coordination, strength, and endurance. When upon the urging of his strict and demanding father he started to take boxing lessons, his "inferiority" was again confirmed as he faced much older boys. In his behavior, too, parents and teachers expected him to act according to his size rather than his age.

Psychophysiological complaints of abdominal pains and vomiting associated with school attendance brought him to the attention of the author. He was able to verbalize his conflict about the school's and parental expectations. His parents and teachers responded well to counseling and were able to adjust their demands to S.'s age and maturity rather than his size and body build. He was encouraged to engage in individual rather than competitive sports and he did well.

E.G., a twelve-year-old girl, was referred because of many school absences, psychosomatic and hysterical complaints, social isolation, and compulsive preoccupation with school work. There were neurotic tendencies and preoccupation with health in both parents. She was seen off and on for a number of years. It was not until she reached fourteen years of age that she was able to verbalize her great concern with her immature body build and absence of menstruation. Much of her isolation was now traced by her to the time of the first interviews when she was entering junior high school and had to expose herself during showers. Many of the girls were then much further developed and the school culture was directed toward social involvement with boys.

Once E. had recognized and admitted to herself her fears about her physical condition, she consulted the corresponding specialists (gynecologist and endocrinologist), accepted her sexual underdevelopment—not without a certain degree of regret and anxiety—and compensated by focusing her efforts toward higher education and a fulfilling career.

Individuation and Separation (School Phobia)

Learning means growing up, but also giving up the comfortably protected childhood position; making new experiences, but also facing the unknown; enjoying new opportunities, but also facing new responsibilities; gaining new privileges, but also assuming new duties; knowing what to do, but also having to make decisions; being able to care and provide for others, but also giving up the protection and care by one's parents, teachers, etc.; knowing right from wrong and acting accordingly, but also losing the privilege of being excused as a child who "doesn't know yet."

It is no wonder, then, that successful learning evokes ambivalent feelings and that these feelings may enhance or hinder the learning process.

Nonlearning means remaining a child, avoiding the responsibilities, duties, and chores of the older child and delaying separation from mother. Not all children consider being the eldest as an advantage.

S.H., age ten, and the eldest of several siblings, demanded to see his birth certificate. When questioned about the reason, he expressed the belief that he was adopted to perform slave duties for the family. The ability to express these feelings as well as the parents' ready recognition and acceptance probably prevented more dramatic attempts at remaining a child, such as regressive behavior or failure to achieve in school.

L.T., a twenty-two-year-old girl who had to drop out of college in her senior year because of a depressive reaction which included a suicidal attempt, was unable to finish her last course to complete the required credits for graduation.

During psychotherapy she was able to recognize that she was not ready to assume the new role in life expected by her parents (and society) after completion of college: job, marriage, and children. She neither felt secure in assuming these responsibilities nor was she willing to give up the comforts of a student life, especially when not attending a prescribed course of study. Once she recognized the "reason" for her inability to complete college and was assured that she would not be expelled from her home and forced to assume responsibilities for which she was not ready, she completed college and continued to engage in psychotherapy to resolve the deeper, much more important causes of her immaturity and dependency.

While some children see school success as a process of growing up and abandoning the status of childhood, older teenagers, confused about their identity (Who am I? What do I want to be? What do my parents want me to be?) and wrestling with the problem of low self-esteem, often see school attendance as a symbol of childhood, inadequacy, absence of self-determination, and lack of maturity. In the lower economic classes the child rarely has the opportunity to see his parents engaged in educational endeavors or his older brother or sister involved in higher education. Quitting school is thus associated with reaching adulthood and maturity irrespective of age and academic achievement.

Thus school failure in one child may be a means of preserving the status of childhood dependency, possibly even in compliance with subconscious parental wishes, while in another child it may be a step toward dropping out of school and working, thus gaining independence and status with his peers.

School phobia, an inhibition to go to school, is a neurotic

symptom usually associated with separation anxiety, although other causes may produce a fear of attending school. The child's behavior may range from "I don't know what it is, but I just don't think I can go to school—maybe on Monday I'll try," to severe panic reactions expressed by "I would rather die!" with screaming and physical resistance to leaving the house, entering school, or letting go of mother. The fear may be converted into psychosomatic symptoms which prevent the child from leaving home (headache, abdominal pains, nausea and vomiting). In school phobia the fear is projected upon "something going on at the school" while in reality it is the inability to separate from mother. This in turn often has its deeper roots in the mother's inability to separate from the child.

A mother, while bringing one of her children to the Clinic because he had been skipping school, brought her thirteen-year-old daughter along because she (the mother) "did not want to come to the Clinic alone." Thus while "trying" to correct truancy in one child, she produced a separation problem in the other child as a result of her own inadequacy.

Another mother, who had a nine o'clock appointment at the Clinic, which the child was attending because of earlier refusal to go to school, found it incomprehensible that the therapist could ask her (the mother) to come alone to the next interview at the same hour: "How would Bertha get to school?" When the girl, standing next to her, assured her that she had discussed this issue with the doctor and it would be all right for her to go to school by herself, the mother, almost in tears, began to question her: "Are you sure you will be all right?" and "Shouldn't I rather take a later appointment and take you to school?"

These mothers, usually very dependent upon their own mothers, never resolved this attachment sufficiently to form a close, meaningful and, at their age, more appropriate attachment to their husbands (Johnson, 1941; Waldfogel, 1954; Estes, 1956). They are dissatisfied with these relationships and in their neurotic search for a solution maintain a very strong attachment to their children. While in the early years this may not be too disturbing to the child and (neurotically) satisfactory to the mother, it becomes very disturbing as the child grows older, wants and is expected by society to leave home to go to school and form new relationships with teachers, schoolmates, and neighbors (Glaser, 1959).

Unresolved dependency of the mother is only one cause for her overattachment to her child. Mother's feelings of rejection toward the child and the ensuing guilt feelings also may lead to overprotection and dependency.

Separation difficulties between mother and child are not the only cause of school phobia, although some authors like to include only separation anxiety into this category. Any fear or discomfort-producing situation at school or on the way to or from school may produce the symptomatology of school phobia. School phobia in adolescence may be a symptom of serious underlying pathology such as masked depression or schizophrenia (see Major Psychiatric Disorders). These are not cases of school phobia *per se,* but school phobia is the predominant symptom at that time.

The treatment of school phobia consists of two phases: After it is established that no rational cause for fear exists and that the child does not suffer from a physical or major mental disorder, an immediate attempt should be made to return the child to school. Verbal pressure, physical assistance, and environmental maneuvers are used. This rapid return is important to avoid secondary effects due to prolonged absence such as academic retardation, shame upon returning, ridicule, etc. Secondly, the underlying problem should be treated. Depending on its depth and duration, this may in some cases be resolved quickly or resolve itself, or may require prolonged psychotherapy for child and mother.

CONFLICTS RELATED TO THE LEARNING PROCESS

Truancy and Delinquency

Truancy is a deliberate absence from school, on a purposeful basis, and not associated with fear projected upon the school or caused by a school-related situation. The child usually plans his absence and may deceive his parents by leaving the house at the regular time and returning after school closing time. He may spend the time in the woods, at the house of a friend whose parents are not at home, in shopping centers, or elsewhere. He often arranges to meet other truants.

While fear of criticism for poor performance or lack of school preparation may play a role, it is mostly lack of motivation, for whatever reason, and the attraction of roaming in freedom that causes the child to be truant. A high degree of underachievement or low ability in relation to expected standards may be associated with lack of motivation.

Some aspects of the current youth culture—the hippie philosophy, the rejection of the standards of the establishment, and the question as to the relevance of the curriculum—give the child at least superficial justification to avoid school: "It don't teach me nothing that I need."

Refusal to learn or attend school may be group compliant behavior. In a delinquent subculture defiance of external authority is the *sine-qua-non* of acceptance. Once the pattern has persisted for some time, it is difficult to give up even with outside assistance. Psychiatric treatment, which is often forced upon the child under threat by the court's authority, is rarely effective. In such youngsters nonachievement and noncompliance with rules is anticipated by peers, teachers, and parents alike. The child is adapted to his subculture and change would mean disloyalty to his friends. It would also mean an uphill fight for acceptance by teachers and even parents who may find it difficult to shed their suspicious and distrustful attitude and thus may see their prophesy of anticipated maladaptation to school fulfilled. In these situations we are dealing essentially with a sociological rather than a psychiatric problem. Mental health personnel are trained to help people adjust, but these children *are* adjusted—unfortunately to an undesirable subgroup.

It is well known that most delinquent children are usually retarded in academic achievement, especially in reading skills. Remedial school programs, although highly desirable, are likely to fail because of the student's lack of motivation or his absence from school altogether. The interaction between intelligence, social factors, and school achievement is reciprocal. A school curriculum geared toward early employment, possibly tied to a concurrent work experience with financial rewards, may return some of these youngsters to the learning process and prevent their seeking income and emotional gratification from delinquent acts.

In many elementary and junior high schools some "shop experience" is interspersed among academic subjects. To the child in the low socioeconomic sector of the population the few shop hours are not enough incentive for school attendance. It seems that if the process were reversed and the child given an early opportunity for training in vocational skills, with academic subjects geared essentially in support of the manual work, his motivation may be raised. For example, mathematics may have little meaning to this type of youngster, but if it were necessary for him to learn basic mathematics to figure out measurements of the item he is constructing, he may become motivated. Similarly, reading might be essential to enable him to follow instructions for a project in which he is interested, thus giving him the incentive for using the tool of reading to complete the project.

Parental attitudes must be analyzed. It is not unusual to find seemingly positively-oriented, middle-class parents sufficiently ambivalent to support the child's behavior overtly or covertly: "I didn't have all these opportunities, and look at me— I made it in life; I started work when I was fourteen."—"We are paying for you and supporting you while you go to school, and you don't take advantage of it." While this may be father's expressed view, the real message more likely is, "I started working at fourteen and paid my parents for room and board; why can't you?"—"What are all these new things you are learning good for anyhow? You don't need to learn that stuff when you work in the factory."

In most situations it is unlikely that these parental attitudes can be changed, and the child is not apt to succeed in changing his patterns of failure and noncompliance while under the influence of the home. Removal from the environment, often under duress and with strong external controls, may be necessary and would have to continue for some time. There is, however, strong resistance on the part of some authorities to this approach. First, it is costly; secondly, it is considered inhumane to remove the young from his parents and home environment, often overlooking the fact that there may really be no functioning home and only an undesirable environment. In addition, the facilities to care for these youngsters have often been severely understaffed, overcrowded, and the staff inadequately trained. The resulting ineffectiveness is then used as argument to discredit their value in rehabilitating some youngsters. Yet workable alternatives have still to be found. Group homes and foster homes are not effective if the child persists in being truant from school and running away from home, or if he has added delinquent behavior to his repertoire of rebellion.

Negativism and Rebellion

In the process of normal emotional growth, the drive for independence is often expressed through rebellious behavior, antagonistic to parental wishes and expectations. What more effective way is there to express such feelings than through opposition to successful schooling, the single most extensive process of molding youth into the image of the adult?

This process can take the form of aggressive, disruptive behavior in the classroom, defiant refusal to do school and home work, truancy or, conversely, compliant behavior with passive resistance to learning. This may be on a conscious level, but more often the resistance to learning is subconscious and the child may sit for hours in front of the book without absorbing the information, or "know all the work at home" and fail the test in school. Some early school dropouts fall into this category. Similarly, the choice of a career in such rebellious youngsters is often determined by the subconscious drive to assert their independence in the form of opposition to father's wishes rather than on the basis of inclination, ability, or even opportunity.

The child is not aware of the dynamics, is not responsive

to direct interpretation, and the parents are helpless in the face of "illogical" behavior. They cannot comprehend that the child's actions are guided by subconscious motives rather than by logical, intellectual considerations.

At times, counseling can change the parents' pushing, demanding, and punitive attitude and can help the youngster to gain enough insight into the dynamics of his actions to enable him to change his course. Often, however, child-parent antagonism has become a way of life, has expanded to antagonism and hostility toward teachers and any representatives of authority, and cannot be altered by short term counseling. This is particularly true when deeper psychosexual conflicts are disturbing the child-parent relationship. Then prolonged psychotherapeutic efforts will be indicated, concurrent with intensive parental counseling or treatment. It may even become necessary to remove the child from his environment into an intensive therapeutic setting (Newman, R. G., 1959; Glaser and Clemmens, 1965).

Frustration and Healthy Curiosity

Curiosity is a necessary ingredient for learning. When curiosity cannot be satisfied, the child becomes frustrated: he wants something he does not have. If the goal is within his reach, he may work for it (learn). If it is too far removed, he may not try, consider the goal out of reach, and give up. He will become disinterested, depressed or negativistic, angry, and/or hostile toward those who do not satisfy his curiosity and alleviate his frustration.

A moderate amount of stress is a necessary stimulus toward optimal performance. Such stress may take the form of anxiety before a test or it may be anxiety produced by the wish to please the teacher or be recognized before the class. Stress beyond an easily tolerable level can become agonizing pain, paralyzing tension or hostile aggressiveness. The skillful teacher will keep the child curious and the object of curiosity within reach. Satisfying such curiosity becomes the reward for searching, studying, learning. To what degree such a healthful balance can be maintained depends to a great extent on the personality, psychological sophistication and human warmth of the teacher.

Negative Influences (Interpersonal Reactions)

Unpleasant, threatening, or severely frustrating experiences associated with the first reading efforts can produce negative conditioning to learning. A hated, severe, or punitive teacher or a parent who approaches the first scholastic efforts with "now the time of play and fun is over" may lay the ground for a negative attitude toward learning in general and reading specifically.

If conflict is suspected between child and teacher, the professional must approach the situation carefully to avoid pitfalls. Is the child's and parents' reaction toward the teacher an accurate appraisal of the teacher's or school's shortcomings? Or is it really a reaction to psychological problems within the child (and/or parents) projected upon the teacher and the school? In the former situation other children in the same classroom should be similarly affected. If this is verified, remediation would have to be directed toward the school situation rather than the child. Counseling of the teacher, further training, or removal of the teacher from the elementary school grades may be indicated. Not every person has the personality characteristics to be a teacher of young children. If such a step is not feasible, the child in question may have to be removed from this class or even school, even though this does not correct the situation for the other children.

However, if the child's reaction toward the teacher is the result of projection, often supported by misguided, overly sympathetic parents whose child "can do no wrong," then his removal from the "threatening" situation will only support his inappropriate projective defenses and teach him that difficulties in school (or elsewhere) can be "resolved" by escape and blaming others. Neither teacher nor parents may be in a position to tackle such a problem alone. Professional assistance is needed by a trained person capable of making objective appraisals and recommendations. Such a professional must be free of obligation toward the school or the child and his parents so that he can make unbiased, practical recommendations.

Among other negative influences one must consider the presence of unusually disturbing children in the classroom. There may be "bullies" or children with strong prejudicial attitudes who may exert their influence toward the target child, either directly or with the assistance of others whom they can rally to their side. Again, it is necessary to assess whether the poor peer relationship is truly caused by external factors, that is, by other children, or whether it is the result of provocative behavior or projection on the part of the child in question.

MAJOR PSYCHIATRIC DISORDERS

Among the many factors that can cause school problems, one must certainly consider major mental illness such as schizophrenia and depression. These conditions are relatively rare in children and can go undetected for some time. Efforts to improve the child's school achievement and force his integration with healthy peers may produce additional stress for the sick child. Psychiatric evaluation and treatment and, if necessary, removal from school and placement in a residential facility may be indicated.

Schizophrenia

Early symptoms of schizophrenia may not be recognized as such. The child may be described as "peculiar," "odd," "absent-minded," "daydreaming," or "trying to be funny" to attract attention or escape the learning task. He frequently displays obsessive-compulsive trends or has shown obsessive-compulsive personality characteristics before schizophrenic symptoms appeared. School personnel should be trained to recognize the child with characteristics which either by their severity, persistence, or the combination of several relatively minor symptoms make the child more than a little different from the majority of children of the same age.

An interesting association between minimal brain dysfunction and schizophrenia has been noted on the basis of longitudinal observations of children with minimal brain dysfunction made in recent years. Organic damage as a possible cause for schizophrenia has been reported years ago. Lauretta Bender stated in 1953 that "the etiological factor which is most important in precipitating the schizophrenic illness is a physiological crisis, such as birth, especially with damage such as anoxia; severe illness or accidents. . . ." However, during the following years the main thrust of investigations was in the psychodynamic area of parent-child interaction.

It seems that now the tide is turning again and the interest in the old question of organicity versus functional influences is being reopened with a more receptive eye toward the organic factors.

Mosher and Feinsilver (1971) in a special report on schizophrenia report several studies which seem to indicate a high incidence of some organic deficit in the early years of schizophrenics. One study demonstrated the resemblance of electrical rhythms, learning patterns, intelligence levels, and certain biochemical characteristics in psychotic and in brain damaged children. Another study found that "neurologically normal, disturbed children generally come from abnormal family situations whereas those with neurological abnormalities have comparatively well adjusted families."

The following case report may illustrate such an observation in the author's experience.

D.S. was first seen at six years of age and described by mother as having had difficulties from birth. Coordination was poor, speech was difficult to understand, there was some delay in motor development, tremors of the hands, and various degrees of hyperkinesis depending on the situation in which he was observed. He and his parents were seen in therapy for the next four years, with some interruptions. The school personnel was assisted by written and verbal communications.

Both parents were college graduates functioning well socially and professionally. Their two older daughters had no difficulties.

The mother had reported vaginal bleeding during the first trimester of pregnancy, and the child had several episodes of very high fever associated with contagious diseases between birth and four years. D. had been seen by several professionals and given varied diagnoses such as cerebral palsy and mental retardation. "He will not develop beyond the mental age of five" was one professional comment. Several I.Q. tests, however, revealed average findings between 90 and 110.

Over the years the child developed enuresis, encopresis, pica, and thumb sucking, for varied periods of time. He was clinging to mother and there were separation difficulties. The mother was considered overprotective which, while undesirable, was seen as a normal reaction in view of the child's handicaps and realistic need for more supervision and assistance. The superior functioning of the older sisters and the contradictory advice by some professionals added to mother's confusion.

Between the age of ten and eighteen the child adjusted marginally in public and private schools, with additional help, especially in reading and speech. At age eighteen he returned to the author with "thoughts of persecution," "watching for signals" and believing that school personnel, students, and his mother were involved with criminal organizations which were threatening him. He felt he had the responsibility to observe and make reports about them. He was very reluctant to take psychotropic medication but participated regularly in psychotherapeutic sessions.

He was able to finish high school (special vocational program) and has recently obtained his first job as rod man on a surveying team. He has learned to dissimulate and hide his delusional ideations and continues in psychotherapy. His awkwardness is quite obvious; he denies hallucinations; and he is struggling to gain independence from his parents and find an adult identity, especially in the sexual area.

Over the years the author has observed several cases of a very similar nature. Questions arise as to etiology. Did the same noxious influence produce two different conditions—minimal brain dysfunction and schizophrenia? Are children with minimal brain dysfunction especially fragile and develop schizophrenia as a result of the added stress they have to endure when living with their handicap? Or are the two conditions unrelated and occurring accidentally in the same child?

Whatever the causative relationship, these children experience severe learning difficulties, at first due to the effects of what seems to be minimal brain dysfunction and later due to the schizophrenic process, or as a result of a combination of these factors.

Mednick states in 1970: "We are, perhaps, now at a point where we can hypothesize that pregnancy and birth complications lead to defective hypocampal functioning which in combination with genetic and environmental factors could conceivably play a vital predisposing role in at least some forms of schizophrenia." He came to the hypothesis after an interesting longitudinal study and a review of the literature on human observations and animal experiments.

Depression

Depression can occur in children and adolescents, but the symptomatology is often different from that observed in adults (Glaser, 1967). Failure to achieve can be a symptom of depression (Wertz, 1963; Silverman, 1959) but so can be acting out and delinquent behavior (Glaser, 1965; Keeler, 1954) or school phobia (Agras, 1959), running away, truancy, or other maladaptive behavior.

A rapid downhill course from a good student in the seventh grade to failing marks in the eighth was the presenting symptom in a thirteen-year-old girl. She considered herself stupid, unable to keep up with her classmates, not liked by parents and siblings. The symptoms occurred at the time of her menarche, and she spent much of the interview time discussing the struggle of her changing identity from a child to an adolescent and future adult. She expressed her guilt for her mother's varicose veins, for which she felt responsible since they had occurred following her mother's pregnancies. She was overly concerned about illness and death and finally was able to express her guilt feelings over her death wishes for members of her family. She admitted at least on one occasion to have looked for pills to kill herself.

The depression, camouflaged by school failure, was not evident to her immediate environment (teacher, school counselor, parents). Her parents, very intelligent professionals, considered her happy and popular and described the family relationship as good.

School failure also was the presenting problem in C.D., a very bright ten and a half-year-old girl. She had had traumatic experiences in foster homes after her mother's divorce and was well aware of the current marital difficulties as well as her stepfather's immature behavior. He had had psychiatric care for depressions. Her attachment to her stepfather was pathologically intense, leading during later years to overt sexual approaches.

Projective tests showed feelings of inadequacy and unfulfilled dependency needs as well as depression. She wanted to be a nurse "to help children in wards who had unhappy lives." When she was fifteen, she showed delinquent behavior in addition to continued academic difficulties. She now verbalized her feelings of being unwanted as demonstrated to her by the biological father's desertion of the family and her subsequent foster home placement. The only person by whom she felt really loved was her stepfather, which created severe incestual conflicts. She considered herself the cause of the current marital difficulties and spoke of depression and suicide. Some of her delinquent behavior gave indication of her self-destructive drive.

In this case, depressive elements and suicidal tendencies were overshadowed by the presenting symptoms of school failure, delinquency, and prominent psychosexual conflicts.

While it is certainly not the educator's responsibility to diagnose these conditions, he can make valuable contributions to the child's developmental progress by recognizing that such a youngster is not "lazy" or "stupid" and by encouraging the parents to seek psychiatric help. At times the teacher may have to call upon the counseling, diagnostic, or administrative services of the school to urge reluctant parents to proceed with further examinations of their child.

CHAPTER V

EDUCATIONAL FACTORS

It is not within the scope of this treatise to discuss educational methodology or philosophy, or remedial approaches or techniques. In this field the reader is referred to specialized literature in education. Here we would like to point out some of the social, psychological, and administrative factors which are influenced directly by various educational approaches and school-associated situations and which, in turn, may lead to, aggravate, or perpetuate learning difficulties in some individuals.

OPEN-SPACE CLASSROOM

The hyperkinetic child has difficulties in sustaining attention and excluding external stimuli, thus in concentrating on his work. He can be helped by small class size and structural devices such as study cubicles which protect him from visual inputs from three sides. Together with the smaller number of children and special design of the classroom, this reduces the noise level and helps him focus on his work.

Recent innovations in some school systems have produced the "open-spaced classroom," large rooms providing study areas for several of the formerly self-contained classes. Evaluation of the possible merits of this new approach will not be possible until several years have passed, and results can be tested objectively after the first enthusiasm of the innovators has been replaced by unbiased assessment.

In the meantime some distractible children are exposed to

an even greater number of opportunities for distraction, and their hyperkinesis is more difficult to control. It seems also that in recent years a larger number of children are reported as hyperkinetic. One may wonder whether some borderline children who may have been able to function in a classroom with thirty children without ever being recognized and labeled as "hyperkinetic" may become overstimulated in the new setting.

HOMOGENEOUS VERSUS HETEROGENEOUS GROUPING (ABILITY GROUPING)

Individual differences in children are too numerous to achieve completely homogeneous grouping, and heterogeneous grouping in the extremes is rarely advocated; however, schools of sufficient size have the choice of placing children of similar level of functioning in a series of fairly homogeneous classes, or of having children on all levels in each classroom.

It has been pointed out that the former method leads to psychological trauma by labeling children of the lower classes as "dummies" and encouraging those of the "smart" classes to become "snobs." While there is validity to this criticism of ability grouping, this disadvantage is not eliminated in the heterogeneous classroom where the smart child always knows the answers, and the "dummy" never does. The question may be raised whether the effect of the constant exposure to these obvious differences may not be more detrimental than if the child learns to adjust to the reality situation which he is going to face in adulthood.

In recent years consideration has been given to placing educable mentally retarded (EMR) children into regular classes in traditional schoolrooms or in open-space (no interior wall) settings. Studies about social acceptability (Gottlieb and Budoff, 1973) have shown that "retarded children in the unwalled school were rejected more often than retarded children in the walled school." Also, "integrated EMR children were rejected more than segregated EMR children." Thus, physical contact alone does not necessarily increase acceptability. The effect of grouping upon the self-concept of the retarded has also been studied widely, but so far research has not led to any unequivocal conclusions.

It is important not to lose sight of the fact that school experiences should be preparations for adult life in the world as it is and not as some may want it to be. It requires no studies to know that unskilled workers with a low educational level hardly ever meet the educated intellectuals in situations other than the hierarchical structure of business or industry, with each accepting his position.

Exempted from these generalizations about school grouping are the rare and expensive situations where children are taught in very small classes of not more than fifteen children, and with adequate staff of a teacher and two aides, where individualization and personal attention are feasible.

Continuous scrutiny of changes in performance and hitherto undetected ability is necessary to recognize the "late bloomer." This is a child who begins to perform on his level of ability only after a number of months or years of slow performance. A school system must be flexible enough to recognize such a child and allow him to transfer from level to level according to his ability and performance. Care must be taken to avoid labeling and categorizing such a child whose intellectual growth follows a different timetable.

SOCIAL PROMOTION

Some children find it traumatic not to be promoted because of underachievement. This is understandable: the child is placed with younger children while his former classmates are promoted; he may not be accepted by the younger group who may label him as the "big stupid kid" even though he may be able to function well academically on this younger level. On the other hand, pushing the child along only on the basis of chronological age presents other problems since his academic underachievement in the same age group becomes progressively more obvious and frustrating. Ideally, schools should have a variety of approaches available, such as retention, promotion, ungraded special classes, and others. Decisions should be made for each child individually, taking into consideration chronological age, size, emotional maturity, degree of academic retardation and intellectual functioning, and the psycho-social educational level of the community where the child attends school.

Acceptance of academic limitations in the child is often more a problem for the adult. Professionals and parents have to consider some of their own biases before they can be of help to the child. It is most difficult for any professional to confront the child as well as his parents with the reality that he is handicapped intellectually or that he has a learning disability which may or may not be corrigible, and that he will have to adjust his current and future life to the handicap rather than struggle with the consequences of denial. These difficulties of confronting the inevitable are not unique to the educator. They are well known to be one of the major problems for the physician who faces the patient with an incurable or fatal disease.

EARLY DETECTION AND REMEDIATION

The hyperactive, acting-out, or generally disturbing child or the child with many absences advertizes his difficulties and sooner or later focuses attention on himself and often receives assistance. Not so the withdrawn, quiet, overly compliant child. Yet the emotional pathology may be more severe in the latter. The child may be just shy, or he may have low self-esteem, be depressed, or even prepsychotic. Yet because of the nature of the reaction and the teacher's attention being forced to the disturbing children, such a child tends to be overlooked. Helping the teacher spot these withdrawn children through special courses in psychology is not sufficient since our systems of delivery of diagnostic and therapeutic services are inadequate in quantity. It only contributes to the frustration of this teacher when the "shy" child she refers is not evaluated promptly, or if treatment recommended is not available because the disruptive child occupies a priority position in treatment.

Silver and Hagin (1972) studied first graders between 1969 and 1971 psychiatrically, neurologically, perceptually, psychologically, and educationally and reevaluated them after therapeutic intervention. They found a rather high percentage of children with various degrees of deviations in the above areas of study. The question arose to what extent these findings constituted normal deviations which may have been self-correcting. It can also be assumed that, had these children been examined in a clinical setting rather than in a survey of a regular school population, many of the findings occurring in fifty percent or more of the children might have been interpreted as signs of pathology. This, incidentally, may be another argument in favor of providing some of the needed services within the school system. Readministration of the educational tests revealed that after intervention this group of children was indistinguishable from the control group or had exceeded them in performance. The important conclusion from the study is that integration of evaluative and therapeutic services in a public school, leading to early case finding and therapeutic intervention, can be effective.

Services of this kind on a large scale are costly and the necessary manpower may not be available at this point. However, it seems that some minimal services which would help to discover some of the handicapped children at an earlier age may still be worthwhile. Classroom observation by a psychologically trained, nonthreatening person may help to identify the child in trouble, shed light on the interaction of a troublemaker with the class and the teacher, and assist the teacher in using approaches which may affect the social and psychological integration of students. A similar approach could be used by a roving educator, who may spot the educationally high risk child and through suggestions to the teacher and/or direct additional help to the child prevent him from becoming an educational casualty.

The importance of early detection of learning problems has been pointed out by Schiffman (1972) who found in a study of 10,000 cases, that if learning disability was diagnosed in second grade, remediation was successful in 82 percent of the cases, while if discovered between sixth and ninth grades, it was successful only in 6 to 11 percent. Early detection and prediction of learning success or failure in school have been studied extensively and many tests have been designed (for instance, De Hirsch, 1966; Meeting Street School Screening Test, 1969).

Recent legislation in Illinois made children between the ages of three and twenty-one with learning disabilities eligible for special educational services. As a result of this legislation the "Learning Disability—Early Childhood Research Project" in Illinois is working on the compilation of evaluative instruments ("Developmental Indicators for the Assessment of Learning") for the identification of potential learning problems in preschool children. It is hoped that this will lead to recommendations for intervention and amelioration of difficulties and to preventive and/or remedial programs.

Thompson (1973), who sees dyslexia and some of the symptoms commonly attributed to brain damage primarily a result of developmental lag, probably on a hereditary basis, emphasizes that "with early recognition and adequate remedial reading instruction, a large majority of dyslexic children attain sufficient ability to read" and ". . . some will find their way around the handicap" even without special tutoring. He collected the names of men of eminence who probably had specific language disability (Thompson, 1973). However, examples of such giants of science as Thomas Edison, Harvey Cushing, Albert Einstein, or Paul Ehrlich should not encourage a wait-and-see attitude for the average child.

CHAPTER VI

THE ROLE OF THE PROFESSIONAL

As seen in the preceding chapters, learning difficulties may be the cause or the consequence of educational, psychological, social, medical, neurological, or psychiatric problems. Preventive, diagnostic, and therapeutic procedures therefore involve professionals in all the above specialties. Depending on the nature of the handicap, which is generally multifactorial, various specialists may be called in and required to work as a team.

The leader of such a team may be the professional who either is initially or predominantly involved with the child and his problems. The choice may depend on the age of the child, on professional interests and attitudes, and on availability. The discipline which the team leader represents is generally less important than his capability to cooperate with and utilize coworkers in other disciplines. He must be able to coordinate and unite their efforts so that the child and his parents can receive clearly defined guidance.

The team leader thus protects the family from contradicting, vacillating, or inconsistent professional advice, while he himself can respect and accept the opinions of other professionals and interpret conflicts of professional opinion without confusing the child and his family. He can present choices available to the child and his family after he has interpreted to them the available facts and anticipated consequences. He should, if possible, not be tied to one specific professional school of thought but should have the flexibility to pursue a course of action best suited to the particular situation and reasonably within the reach of the family.

The potential pitfalls of pursuing a specific therapeutic school are illustrated in the following case.

A mildly retarded boy was referred because of school diffi- culties, both academically and in behavior, and disobedience and negativism at home. The preferred mode of operation of the previously treating psychiatrist was family therapy; and since there was a conflict between child and parents he felt justified in pursuing this approach. At the time of consultation it became clear that he had not addressed himself to the issue of mental retardation. Neither did he know the level of functioning, nor was the matter ever discussed in the family sessions because of the presence of the child. Thus he could not deal with the issue of parental awareness and acceptance of the handicap.

The child needed a psycho-educational assessment. The findings revealed that for his intellectual level as measured by standardized tests, rather than by clinical impression, his academic standing was appropriate. He was mentally limited but not academically retarded in relation to his capacity. The next sessions were scheduled with the parents alone to help them understand and accept the child's intellectual deficit and lower their demands as well as their expectations for the future. Subsequently appropriate school placement was secured. After these fundamental steps, additional intra-family conflicts could be approached in joint sessions between parents and child (family therapy).

Recommendations for psychiatric treatment or educational remediation should be realistic with regard to available resources. This does not mean that optimal methods or approaches should not be stated as needed, but parents and child, depending on age, should also receive recommendations which they can real- istically expect to follow. "Ivory tower" idealistic recommenda- tions are frustrating to parents who are then apt to spend their time and energy in searching for unavailable resources and lobbying for yet to be provided facilities while their child receives no help during the crucial developmental years. It would be equally inappropriate to limit our professional advice to minimal approaches because they are readily available or inexpensive. The parents must know the entire spectrum of needed and available resources. Progress in programs and facilities in such areas as learning disabilities and mental retardation has come about more as a result of lobbying efforts of parental organizations than through the direct efforts of professionals. These parents would not have been in the position to pressure for the resources had they not been frankly appraised of what could be done for their child *if* appropriate facilities were available.

It is of the greatest importance that continued or repeated professional assistance be available throughout the years. The team leader in particular should be able to remain available to the child and the family, be capable of adapting his approaches to the changing needs of the developing young person, and be prepared to vary the course of action if certain therapeutic or remedial methods fail to achieve the desired results. Parents who may have the knowledge and ability to cope with a handicapping condition in one phase of the child's development may need continued education and guidance as new problems arise.

The high degree of mobility of our population and the 'clinic' approach often do not allow for continuity of treatment. The opinions of changing clinic personnel may vary and their knowledge of the case depends upon often sparsely written records or records so voluminous that they become impractical for service.

The private pediatrician or child psychiatrist may be in the best position to serve as the link throughout the child's years of development. He may serve as the "team leader," coordinating and interpreting the services of all the specialists involved in the diagnostic and therapeutic approaches. He should be knowledgeable of changing resources in the community and willing to undertake the taxing job of regulating and supervising medication in the child with neurological or psychological disorders. He should also be available to school personnel for interpretation and suggestions.

While a multidisciplinary approach to learning disorders is

essential, one must not lose sight of the fact that, after recognized medical, psychological, and social defects are corrected, the prime responsibility for the specific remediation of the learning or reading problems remains the prerogative of the educator. It is the classroom teacher who must deal with the child's learning deficiency on a daily basis, and it is the special educator who has the expertise to institute the necessary corrective educational programs.

CHAPTER VII

GLIMPSES INTO THE FUTURE

Dreams: Some more, some less
fantastic—some may even come
true in our lifetime.

T HE CURRENT STATE of the art with respect to learning difficulties leaves many problems unsolved and needs and challenges
unmet. Research is needed in all areas and may lead to answers
to some of the questions. But whether the implementation of
programs developed on the basis of research findings will produce
the expected results without undesirable and unexpected side
effects can be ascertained only after practical application. We
are, after all, dealing with very complex factors when we talk
about learning and learning problems. Involved are not only
educators, educational systems and programs, and our entire
school age population, but in a wider sense the impact of our
overall educational efforts upon every phase of the individual's
adult life and indirectly the functioning of the country as a whole.

In view of such complexity it would seem advisable that
any new ideas be introduced cautiously and in a limited scope
before large scale investments and major changes are imple-
mented. Granted that traditional teaching methods have not
produced the best possible results, they have nevertheless served
our current generation of adults and were at one time considered
the latest innovations.

However, new discoveries offer the opportunity for new
approaches, changes in culture and technology make new

demands, and we must attempt to meet these challenges if we are to prepare the coming generation for the tasks ahead.

In the following some thoughts and ideas are presented about the directions which future progress may take.

NEUROCHEMISTRY

It is difficult and at times impossible to translate experimental findings in animals onto the human organism in areas where the two species are most divergent: intellect, language, symbolization, and so on. But some deductions can be made, and naturally occurring biochemical abnormalities in man shed some light on the chemistry of brain development and learning. Certain varieties of mental deficiency (learning defects) are based on neurochemical disorders. A large number of amino acid, carbohydrate, and lipid disorders have been identified in children with such defects. Furthermore, "neurochemists are beginning to observe developmental points at which the addition of a boost to the neurochemical development of the normal brain might produce great benefits to its later functioning. . . . The human is born with only approximately 1/4th of the brain weight, and the remaining 3/4th are synthesized in the first six years of life. . . . There is correlation between the biochemical development, the development of the electrical activity of the brain, and the development of behavioral responses and ability" (Bogoch, 1973).

The effects of malnutrition, hypoxia, viral attacks, and hormonal influences vary depending on the developmental phase of the brain at which the noxious influence or deprivation occurs. While it can be demonstrated that malnutrition during the first years of life will affect brain size and DNA content of the brain in human infants, these nutritional influences cannot be separated from other biological, sociological, or psychological variables. Conclusions can therefore be only suggestive. Experiments with pigeons have shown that glycoproteins affect the development of the brain and seem to influence learning ability. Many drugs or substances which naturally occur in food are under investigation. McGaugh (1971) studied the influence of drugs upon memory in mice. Rosenzweig *et al.* (1971) demonstrated quantitative and chemical brain changes in animals due to environmental factors, and there have been many other studies attempting to show causative relationships between biochemical factors and brain functioning.

Based on these current investigations, is it not conceivable that in the future we may be able to enhance artificially the development of the young brain? Or to improve certain learning functions in the developed brain? Or that we could eventually correct learning disorders by the judicious use of nonaddictive safe medications?

MATURATION AND SCHOOL ONSET

Would a delay of one year in reading instruction in our public school systems reduce the number of reading problems and learning casualties?

Ages five to seven seems to be the critical period in the child's development with regard to reading readiness. The chronological age at the time the child enters school can vary as much as twelve months within each class (see Chapter I). The rate of maturation in boys and girls is different in all developmental areas. In addition, there are considerable individual variations. Thus every September when school opens we find a rather heterogeneous group of children with regard to reading readiness. The above takes into account only the physiological differences, without even considering sociological and cultural influences which further contribute to the vast differences in receptiveness to learning.

Thus might it not be possible that more children would benefit—or perhaps fewer children would suffer—if our public schools would begin to teach reading to children at age seven rather than six? Certainly there would be children whose opportunity to learn would be delayed unnecessarily. But on the other hand we should find considerably fewer children physiologically not ready to read and thus subject to the well known traumatic experiences.

We might compare such a trend of thought to public health

approaches which are based on the premise of producing the most good for most people, even though there may be discomfort to some and a risk of serious damage to a very few. This ratio of risk of damage to benefit can be further reduced by limiting public health measures to certain selected population subgroups which are particularly high at risk. For instance, smallpox vaccination is not without danger, yet the risk was considered justified as long as thousands of deaths occurred as a result of the disease. Once smallpox was virtually eliminated from most countries, even the small risk of vaccination was no longer justified for the general population. Yet those who travel to countries where the disease still occurs, or those who work in hospitals which may receive patients afflicted with smallpox are not only in danger themselves but present a danger to the public at large. Thus the danger involved in the vaccination itself is justified for this high-risk group, both in the interest of the individual as well as the public.

We might consider utilizing such a selective approach by delaying the beginning of reading instruction only in areas where the incidence of children not ready for the task is very high. Some teachers even now find that they must spend considerably more time on reading readiness training with first graders when the majority of students is not ready for the task of reading. In such situations would it not be better for the majority of children if an overall policy would delay the beginning of reading instruction for all children until second grade?

Ideally, one should strive for individualization and allow each child to proceed at his own optimal rate of learning, whether this means learning to read as early as age four or as late as age eight. However, this would produce classes of children uneven in size and social maturity and this in turn would lead to other difficulties which, as present thinking goes, outweigh the problems produced by the currently favored policy of starting reading instruction based on chronological age.

Finding some acceptable compromise solution for our mass public education system is a challenge which, although recognized, will occupy educational experts for a long time to come.

VALUES, INDUSTRIALIZATION, AUTOMATION,
AND ECONOMIC MOTIVATION

Values

Educational and vocational choices are influenced by many subjective considerations which are not always in the best interest of the child. The competitive spirit of some parents with regard to their children's careers, the high value placed on academic achievement, and the low recognition afforded manual labor make it almost impossible to reach objective decisions based on ability, attained maturity, individual interest, and job opportunities. In certain circles, objective and educationally sound decisions to direct a child at an early age toward learning manual skills and on-the-job training (apprenticeship training) may have damaging effects upon social status and self-esteem.

One has to consider seriously whether the effects of such stigmatization would not be outweighed by the hardship of the educational struggle in a child who may not be capable of following the prescribed academic curriculum at a standard schedule. Learning failure due to inappropriate choice or unavailability of alternative educational and training opportunities is frequent. Unfortunately these issues are clouded further by ethnic, racial, and political considerations which cannot be ignored.

Could we expect to influence middle class attitudes toward certain occupations and change the status assigned to some jobs by reeducational programs in the schools, directed toward children as well as parents? Efforts would probably have to extend beyond schools and make use of mass media in order to effect value changes in large sections of the population. There might be some difficulty in reconciling such efforts with goals for some youngsters in the working class in families of unskilled workers who do not have a college background. Here it is our endeavor to encourage the capable child to continue his academic education beyond high school. While this does not present a difficulty on an individual basis and maybe not even in the neighborhood school, it would be difficult through mass media to extol the virtues of manual skills for the nonacademically oriented middle class child and at the same time praise the benefits of a college education for the bright child in the working class. In any event, such large-scale shifts in educational emphasis would necessitate vast expansion of training facilities, both in numbers and in diversity of program offerings.

Industrialization and Automation

Issues of vocational preference are closely tied to some perhaps irreversible changes in our production system. The time is past when the skilled craftsman took a piece of wood and through his skill and labor fashioned a finished product of which he could be proud, or when the farmer gathered the seeds at the end of the season and replanted them and nurtured them until they ripened into fruit which he then offered for sale to the hungry consumers.

Man has become a machine operator, familiar only with one of the intermediate steps in the long process of production, never enjoying the gratification of creating a product from beginning to end and seeing the fruits of his labor. Our mechanized, efficient, and impersonal production processes have deprived most workers of this source of satisfaction. Those who have the opportunity to view the entire process, enjoy its efficiency, and earn the economic rewards are administrators (executives) who are, however, removed from the production process itself and observe it only from their offices on paper reports and graphs. Because of the high financial rewards in these positions and the power of decision-making vested in them, these executives are not seen as part of the production team.

The worker does not work *with* the executive to produce what the public needs but he works *for* the manager and for the profit of the owners. He has no influence on the production process as a whole, nor does he see any direct connection between the quality of his labor, the profit for the company, and the benefits for himself. Thus he feels alienated from the entire system. He views himself as an insignificant extension of the machine, with no opportunity to utilize any skill or knowledge he may have acquired in school.

What is the relevance for such a person of the many years

spent in school, and what is the connection between the subjects he studied and his current and possibly lifelong occupation as an unskilled assembly line operator? Why should his child have to go through this same process of academic learning which has become meaningless to the father? Yet father's work has been well paid, job security has been fairly high, and he has been able to provide many of the luxuries of life the children enjoy. Why, then, should these children want to delay their material rewards by spending more years in school for a higher education which for them is of very questionable value?

Some small attempts have been made to correct the effects of alienation at least partially by restructuring assembly line processes so as to have teams of men working on certain production steps from beginning to end, thus giving them the opportunity to enjoy the pride of seeing a finished or at least partially finished, recognizable product. Similarly, various profit sharing plans have attempted to give the worker a financial interest in the quality of his work. Whether these changes will produce the desired effects remains yet to be seen.

Economic Motivation

The overall shift of values toward material and pleasure-oriented rewards in our society has also had its impact upon our youth's motivation to pursue intellectual (school-oriented) endeavors which do not lead to the goals cherished by a majority of the adult society.

It is possible to conceive, and certainly permissible to dream, that a shift of emphasis from the technological and material development of our society toward social, cultural, and intellectual values may take place and that certain crafts and services would regain the respectability they once had. Expert craftsmanship can then become again a desirable goal for a lifelong occupation and not a poor second choice for those who fail in academic studies. Our educational resources would not only have to adapt to this process but ideally should be designed to stimulate students toward pursuing such goals. We may then even see these young people motivated to learn mathematics, reading, or drawing as related to the craft they have chosen as their career, with realistic expectations of material, social, and personal rewards.

SIMPLIFICATION OF LANGUAGE

It is difficult to estimate how much economy in learning could be effected if the written English language now in use could be modified to bring spelling closer to pronunciation. Spontaneous developmental changes of English have occurred over the centuries (hath, thou). Could we conceive of a generally accepted, deliberate process to simplify our written language and make it more phonetic (night—nite)? Some attempts in this direction have already been made, as for instance with the Initial Teaching Alphabet which has been tried in some school systems, with as yet questionable results.

It has been said that when we replace our current measuring system with the metric system, teaching of mathematics in our schools could be shortened by as much as two years. Could the same apply to simplifications in reading, writing, and spelling? This should not imply that a modification of spelling and reduction of discrepancies in pronunciation would eliminate specific reading disability, but it could reduce the difficulty which normal and dyslexic children experience in acquiring reading and spelling skills. Observation that dyslexic children in English-speaking countries have relatively greater and more persistent difficulties in spelling than, for instance, Czech children lends support to this hypothesis. If the child can acquire reading and spelling skills in less time and with less effort, more of his energy would be freed for learning subject matter.

Makita (1968) studied reading disability in Japan and visited countries the world over. He writes that "60 percent of reading disability in the world is in English speaking countries." German speaking countries are next, in Italy and Spain the incidence is lower, and in Japan it is rare. He explains that "English exceeds by far . . . in the number of words in which irregular or unstable relationships exist between spelling and pronunciation" . . . "Japanese Kana stands in extreme contrast to English." He concedes, however, that his survey in Japan was made by questionnaire and that poor readers may be underreported for various reasons. Precise, controlled, statistical studies between countries may never be feasible because it may be impossible to control for major variables such as teaching methods, school philosophy, and cultural differences.

EXPANSION OF PREVENTIVE MEASURES

The first line of defense against school failure is prevention. Early detection of high-risk children with potential school difficulties in the academic or emotional sphere has been attempted. However, preventive and remedial facilities are still scarce, out of reach for some, and underutilized by others. Indifference, unawareness, denial, and fear of stigmatization on the part of parents should be counteracted by vigorous adult education programs. Parent training projects and school programs geared to preparing today's teenagers for future parenthood may bring about improvement in child rearing practices in future generations and provide the young with the stimulation and motivation needed to succeed in the educational process.

Unawareness, indifference, or neglect can also be observed in professionals who may be in a position to identify the child with potential difficulties at an early age and initiate remediation. Our educational efforts in this direction will need to be extended to professional schools and training centers in order to reach all those preparing for careers in areas involving health and education of the young.

Some attempts at early identification and remediation for the high-risk or troubled child have been described under educational factors (see Chapter V). An expansion of such services is costly in money and manpower now but may prove highly profitable in the long run when these children reach adulthood. Some of the preventive and remedial services that are already under way are nationwide and federally funded, while others are locally sponsored; some are experimental to determine effectiveness, while others seem to have been recognized as at least partially effective. All these programs will need continued support, expansion and modification in order to reach eventually all children in need of these services.

Project Head Start, the largest and most ambitious program to date, offers deprived preschoolers educational and emotional preparation before entering the school system. In addition, it provides complete health care for the children, while their parents are offered instruction in nutrition, child rearing practices and other areas affecting their children's welfare directly and indirectly. The project was started on a large scale, with little prior experimentation, and the validity of the instruments used for measuring its effectiveness has been subject to question. Nevertheless it seems that programs such as the year long Project Head Start are effective in raising the level of functioning of children in disadvantaged areas. If this gain can be sustained by continued intensified educational efforts such as the Follow-Through program, we may find in the coming years a population better prepared to accept the challenges of our technological development (Hellmuth, 1968, 1970).

Day Care Centers for the poor or children of working mothers aim to provide stimulation and socialization for the children while freeing their mothers to work, thus allowing them to lead a more self-respecting and self-directing life than those who have to depend on public support.

In many urban centers local programs have been developed with varied emphases and of different sizes. Often they are only pilot or experimental programs of limited scope and duration. Others—such as the Children's Guild in Baltimore—have existed for years and have offered therapeutic educational programs to troubled preschool children as well as counseling to their mothers.

Although attempts at detection and remediation of educational or emotional deficits in early childhood are numerous, they still affect only a small number of the total child population. Let us hope that popular demand and governmental response will in the future lead to provision of adequate services designed to prevent or correct the damages and deprivations some children are subjected to. While the effort and the expense will be with this generation, the fruits may be plentiful with the next.

BIBLIOGRAPHY

No ATTEMPT HAS been made to make this list of references comprehensive, nor have publications been selected according to their importance. The goal rather was to provide the reader interested in a specific subject with a readily available reference source to enable him to study the individual subject in greater depth, or to find documentation of a statement or opinion voiced in the text.

Agras, S.: The Relationship of School Phobia to Childhood Depression. *Am J Psychiatry, 116*:533, 1959.

Anastasi, Anne: *Psychological Testing,* Third Edition. New York: MacMillan Co., 1968.

Bender, Lauretta: Childhood Schizophrenia. *The Psychiatric Quarterly,* New York State Department of Mental Hygiene, October, 1953.

Bentzen, F.: Sex Ratios in Learning and Behavior Disorders. *Am J Orthopsychiatry, 23*:92, 1963.

Birch, Herbert G.: *A Selected Bibliography on Brain-Damaged Children.* The Woods School and Residential Treatment Center, Langhorne, Pa., 1964.

Bogoch, Samuel: Neurochemical Changes Associated with Learning. From an address at the Annual Meeting of the Association for Children with Learning Disabilities, Detroit, March, 1973, and Personal Communication.

Clemmens, Raymond L., and Glaser, Kurt: Specific Learning Disabilities, I. Medical Aspects. *Clinical Pediatrics, 6*:481-486, August, 1967.

DeHirsch, Katrina; Jansky, Jeannette J., and Langford, William S.: *Predicting Reading Failure.* New York: Harper & Row, 1966.

Denhoff, Eric; Siqueland, Marian L.; Komich, M. Patricia, and Hainsworth, Peter K.: Developmental and Predictive Characteristics of Items from the Meeting Street School Screening Test. *Developmental Medicine and Child Neurology, 10*:220-232, 1968.

DIAL—Developmental Indicators for the Assessment of Learning: Described in *Learning Disabilities/Early Childhood Research Project.* Office of Superintendent of Public Instruction, State of Illinois, Annual Report, August 31, 1972.

Drillien, C. M.: A Longitudinal Study of the Growth and Development of Prematurely and Maturely Born Children. *Archives of Diseases of Childhood, 36*:233, 1961.

Drillien, C. M.: Obstetric Hazard, Mental Retardation and Behaviour Disturbance in Primary School. *Develop Med Child Neurol,* 5:3, 1963.

Eisenberg, Leon: Reading Retardation: I. Psychiatric and Sociologic Aspects. *Pediatrics,* 37:352, 1966.

Estes, H. R.; Haylett, C. H., and Johnson, A. M.: Separation Anxiety. *Am J Psychotherapy,* 10:682, 1956.

Friedman, M.: Some Aspects of Cultural Deprivation. *Pathways in Child Guidance,* Bureau of Child Guidance, Board of Education of the City of New York, 4:1, 1962.

Gerstmann, J. :Fingeragnosie: Eine umschriebene Stoerung der Orientierung am eigenen Koerper. *Wiener Klinische Wochenschrift,* 37:1010-1012, 1924.

Gerstmann, J.: Syndrome of Finger Agnosia, Disorientation for Right and Left, Agraphia and Acalculia. *Archives of Neurology and Psychiatry,* 44:398-408, August 1940.

Glaser, Kurt and Eisenberg, Leon: Maternal Deprivation. *Pediatrics,* 18:626-642, 1956.

Glaser, Kurt: School Phobia and Related Conditions. *Pediatrics,* 23:371-383, 1959.

Glaser, Kurt: Conflicts and Rebellion during Adolescence. *Pediatrics,* 26:839-845, 1960.

Glaser, Kurt, and Clemmens, Raymond L.: School Failure. *Pediatrics,* 35:128-141, 1965.

Glaser, Kurt: Suicide in Children and Adolescents. *Acting Out—Theoretical and Clinical Aspects,* edited by Lawrence Edwin Abt and Stuart L. Weissman. New York: Grune & Stratton, 1965.

Glaser, Kurt: Masked Depression in Children and Adolescents. *Am J of Psychotherapy,* 21:565-574, 1967.

Glaser, Kurt and Clemmens, Raymond L.: Specific Learning Disabilities, II. Psychosocial Aspects. *Clinical Pediatrics,* 6:487-491, August, 1967.

Goldberg, Herman K. and Schiffman, Gilbert B.: *Dyslexia: Problems of Reading Disabilities.* New York: Grune & Stratton, 1972.

Goldstein, K.: *The Organism—A Holistic Approach to Biology.* New York: American Book Company, 1939.

Gottlieb, J. and Budoff, M.: Social Acceptability of Retarded Children in Nongraded Schools Differing in Architecture. *Am J Mental Deficiency,* 78:15-19, 1973.

Hallgren, B.: Specific Dyslexia: A Clinical and Genetic Study. *Acta Psychiat Neurol Supplement,* Vol. 65, 1960.

Hellmuth, Jerome, (Ed.): *Disadvantaged Child, Vol. 2: Head Start and Early Intervention.* Seattle, Wash.: Special Child Publications, 1968.

Hellmuth, Jerome (Ed.): *Disadvantaged Child, Vol. 3; Compensatory Education—A National Debate.* New York: Brunner Mazel. 1970.

Hermann, K. and Norrie, E.: Is Congenital Word-Blindness a Hereditary Type of Gerstmann's Syndrome? *Psychiat Neurol* (Basel), 136:59, 1958.

Hermann, K.: *Reading Disability*: *A Medical Study of Word-Blindness and Related Handicaps*. Springfield, Ill.: Charles C Thomas, 1959.

Johnson, A. M.; Falstein, E. I.; Szurek, S. A., and Svendsen, M.: School Phobia. *Am J Orthopsychiatry, 11*:702-711, 1941.

Joint Organizational Statement—American Academy of Pediatrics, American Academy of Ophthalmology and Otolaryngology, and the American Association of Ophthalmology: The Eye and Learning Disabilities. *Pediatrics, 49*:454-455, March, 1972.

Jones, H.: *The Environment and Mental Development—Manual in Child Psychology*. New York: Wiley, 1954.

Kahn, E. and Cohen, L. H.: Organic Drivenness: A Brain-stem Syndrome and an Experience. *New England Journal of Medicine, 210*:748-756, 1934.

Kanner, Leo: The Integrative Aspect of Ability. *Acta Paedopsychiatrica, 38*:134-144, 1971.

Kanner, Leo: *Child Psychiatry*. 4th ed. Springfield, Ill.: Charles C Thomas, 1972.

Kawi, A. and Pasamanick, B.: Prenatal and Paranatal Factors in Children with Reading Disorders. *Monogr Soc Research Child Development, 24*:4, 1959.

Keeler, W. R.: Children's Reactions to the Death of a Parent. *Depression*. Edited by P. H. Hoch and J. Zubin. New York: Grune & Stratton, 1954.

Keogh, Barbara K.: Optometric Vision Training Programs for Learning Disability Children: Review of Issues and Research. *Journal of Learning Disabilities*, In Press.

McDill, Edward L.; McDill, Mary S., and Sprehe, J. Timothy: *Strategies for Success in Compensatory Education*: *An Appraisal of Evaluation Research*. Baltimore: Johns Hopkins Press, 1969.

McGaugh, James L.: Biological Bases of Memory. *The Mental Health of the Child*. Program Reports of the National Institute of Mental Health. Edited by Julius Segal. Public Health Service Publication No. 2168, Washington, D.C., 1971.

McLeod, John: "It's the same the whole world over . . ." Symposium on Dyslexia International. *Bulletin of the Orton Society, 22*:98-103, 1972.

Makita, K.: The Rarity of Reading Disability in Japanese Children. *Am J Orthopsychiatry, 38*:599-614, 1968.

Matejcek, Zdenek: Dyslexia: Diagnostic and Treatment Findings and Recommendations. *Bulletin of the Orton Society, 21*:53-63, 1971.

Mednick, Sarnoff, A.: Breakdown in Individuals at High Risk for Schizophrenia: Possible Predispositional Perinatal Factors. *Mental Hygiene, 54*:50-63, January, 1970.

Meeting Street School Monograph: *Early Identification of Children with Learning Disabilities*. Meeting Street School, Children's Rehabilitation Center, Providence, R.I., 1969.

Money, John, (Ed.): *Reading Disability*: *Progress and Research Needs in Dyslexia*. Baltimore: The Johns Hopkins Press, 1962.

Mosher, Loren R. and Feinsilver, David: *Special Report: Schizophrenia.* U.S. Department of Health, Education, and Welfare, National Institute of Mental Health, 1971.

Newman, C. Janet; Dember, Cynthia Fox, and Krug, Othilda: "He Can But He Won't"—A Psychodynamic Study of So-called "Gifted Under-achievers." *The Psychoanalytic Study of the Child,* 28:83-129, 1973.

Newman, R. G.: Assessment of Progress in the Treatment of Hyper-aggressive Children with Learning Disturbance Within a School Setting. *Amer J Orthopsychiatry,* 29:633, 1959.

Office of Child Development—Report of Conference on the Use of Stimulant Drugs in the Treatment of Behaviorally Disturbed Young School Children, January 11-12, 1971: Department of Health, Education, and Welfare, Washington, D.C., 1971.

O'Malley, J. E. and Eisenberg, L.: The Hyperkinetic Syndrome. *Seminars in Psychiatry,* 5:95, 1973.

Pasamanick, B., and Lilienfeld, A. M.: Pregnancy Experience and the Development of Behavior Disorders in Children. *Amer J Psychiatry, 112:*8, 1956.

Prechtl, Heinz F. R.: Reading Difficulties as a Neurological Problem in Childhood. *Reading Disability: Progress and Research Needs in Dys-lexia,* Edited by John Money. Baltimore: The Johns Hopkins Press, 1962. pp. 187-193.

Rabinovitch, Ralph D.: Dyslexia: Psychiatric Considerations, in *Reading Disability: Progress and Research Needs in Dyslexia,* Edited by John Money. Baltimore: The Johns Hopkins Press, 1962, pp. 73-79.

Rapaport, D.: *Diagnostic Psychological Testing,* Volume I. Chicago: Year-book Publications, 1945.

Rosenberg, Leon A.: A Culture-Fair Instrument for Intellectual Assess-ment. *Disadvantaged Child, Volume 2: Head Start and Early Inter-vention,* edited by Jerome Hellmuth. Seattle, Wash.: Special Child Publications, 1968.

Rosenberg, Leon A.: Achievement Motivation in Young Children: I. An Evaluation of a Community Intervention Program, II. The Role of the Quality of Adult Behavior. Mimeographed Progress Report, 1973. (Also Personal Communication)

Rosenzweig, M. R.; Bennett, E. L.; Krech, D., and Diamond, M. C.: The Physiological Imprint of Learning. *The Mental Health of the Child,* Program Reports of the National Institute of Mental Health, Wash-ington, D.C., 1971.

Rutter, Michael; Graham, Philip, and Birch, Herbert G.: Interrelations Between the Choreiform Syndrome, Reading Disability and Psychiatric Disorder in Children of 8-11 Years. *Developmental Medicine and Child Neurology,* 8:149-159, 1966.

Schiffman, G. and Clemmens, R.: Observations on Children with Severe Reading Problems, Learning Disorders. Seattle, Washington, Special Child Publications, 1966. Quoted in *Dyslexia—Problems of Reading*

Disabilities by Goldberg, Herman K. and Schiffman, Gilbert B., New York: Grune & Stratton, 1972, p. 25 f.

Schnackenberg, R. C.: Caffeine as a Substitute for Schedule II Stimulants in Hyperkinetic Children. *Am J Psychiatry, 130*:796, 1973.

Silver, Archie A., and Hagin. Rosa A.: Profile of a First Grade—A Basis for Preventive Psychiatry. *Journal of the Am Academy of Child Psychiatry, 11*:645-674, 1972.

Silverman, J. S.; Fite, M. W., and Mosher, M. M.: Clinical Findings in Reading Disability Children—Special Cases of Intellectual Inhibition. *Am J Orthopsychiatry, 29*:298, 1959.

Simmons, James E.: The Impact of the Family and Home Environment on the Performance of the School Child. *Journal of the Indiana State Medical Association,* June, 1959, pp. 963-967.

Strauss, A. A. and Lehtinen, E. L.: *Psychopathology and Education of the Brain-Injured Child.* New York: Grune & Stratton, 1950.

Thompson, L. J.: Learning Disabilities: An Overview. *Am J Psychiatry, 130*:393-399, 1973.

Waldfogel, S.; Hahn, P. B., and Gardner, G. E.: A Study of School Phobia in Children. *J Nerv & Ment Diseases, 120*:399, 1954.

Wertz, F. J.: Adolescent Underachievers—Evaluating Psychodynamic and Environmental Stresses. *N.Y. State Medical Journal, 63*:3524, 1963.

Wetzel, Karl H.; Welcher, Doris W., and Mellits, E. David: The Possibility of Overdiagnosing Brain Dysfunction From a Single Administration of the Bender Gestalt Test. *The Johns Hopkins Medical Journal, 129*:6-9, July, 1971.

White, Sheldon H.: The National Impact Study of Head Start. in *Disadvantaged Child, Volume 3: Compensatory Education—A National Debate,* Edited by Jerome Hellmuth. New York: Brunner/Mazel, 1970.

Wolff, Peter H. and Hurwitz, Irving: The Choreiform Syndrome. *Developmental Medicine and Child Neurology, 8*:160-165, April, 1966.

INDEX

A

Ability grouping, 63
Academic achievement, 76
Academic limitations
  acceptance of, 65
Academic retardation (*see* Retardation)
Acalculia, 10
Acting-out child, 65
Age differences, chronological, 7
Aggressiveness, aggressive behavior, 4,
  12, 54, 55
Agraphia, 10
Alienation, 77, 78
Amphetamines, 14
Anemia, 5
Antidepressants, 14
Anxiety
  and absence from school, 44
  as cause of overactivity, 11
  as consequence of learning disorders,
    6
  separation, 49, 51
  in specific reading disability, 17
  and stress, 55
  and tranquilizers, 14
Apprenticeship training, 76
Articulation disorders, 9
Assortative mating, 27
Assortative migration, 27, 30
Attention-getting mechanisms, 4
Attention span, short, 8, 10
Auditory handicap, 3
Automation, 76-78
Awkwardness, 17

B

Behavior (*see* specific behavior)
Bender Gestalt Test, 7, 9, 17

Biochemical abnormalities, 73
Biochemical irregularities, 10
Brain damage (*see* Minimal Brain
  Dysfunction)
Brain dysfunction, 7

C

Car accidents, 10
Categorization
  rebellion against, 42
Central nervous system disorders,
  minimal (*see* Minimal Brain
  Dysfunction)
Cerebral development, 10
Cerebral palsy, 29, 58
Chemical brain changes, 74
Child rearing practices, 6, 80
Choreiform movements, 10
Chronic illness, 5, 6
Coffee, in Minimal Brain Dysfunction,
  14
Competitiveness, 33
Compulsion (compulsive), 29, 33, 47
Concreteness of thought, 8
Congenital word blindness, 16
Counseling (*see* individual chapters)
Crisis situations
  in classroom, 15
Cross-eyedness, 6
Cultural differences, 80
Cultural factors
  and education, 36
  influencing IQ test results, 24
  psychological impact of, 40
Cultural influences, 39, 74
Culture changes
  and new approaches, 72
Culture, primitive
  and intellectual inadequacy, 26

Culture-free tests (culture-fair tests), 23

Curriculum, school
adaptation for deprived children, 38, 39
for gifted children, 30

D

Day care centers, 24, 81
Daydreaming, 4, 44, 57
Defenses (defense reactions)
acting out, 28
avoidance, 12, 28, 39
escape, 39, 56
hostility, 12
projection, 56
Defiant behavior, 12
Delinquency, 51-54
and depression, 60, 61
Delinquent subculture, 52
Dependency, childhood, 49
Dependency, unresolved
of mother, 51
Dependency needs
unfulfilled, 61
Depression, masked, 51
Depression, 57
as cause of school problems, 60, 61
and early detection, 65
Depressive reaction, 49
Deprivation
cultural, 38
sensory, 4
stimulus, 4
Destructive behavior, 12
Detection, early, 19, 65-67, 80
Developmental
assessment, 26
difference, 7
lag, 67
Directionality, disorientation in, 10
Distractibility, 8, 9
Distracting factors
affecting school performance, 37
Domestic conflicts, 45

Dropouts, 54
Drug abuse, 42
Drugs, stimulant, 14
Dyslexia
coexisting with mild mental retardation, 26
and developmental lag, 67
in different languages, 79, 80
and English spelling, 20
and genetic factors, 16
and Gerstmann Syndrome, 10
in gifted child, 31
Dyslexia, developmental
incidence, 20
Dyslexic children
and phonetic spelling, 20, 79

E

Early detection (identification), 19, 65-67, 80
Economic factors
affecting school attendance, 37
Educational choices, 76
Electroencephalographic findings, 9
Encephalitis, 10
Environmental deprivation, 24
Environmental factors, 60
Enzymatic irregularities, 10
Epidemiological study
of reading disabilities, 18
Escape
through drug abuse, 42

F

Family composition
changes in, 45
Family mobility, 32
Fatigue, chronic, 6
Fine motor coordination, 17
Finger agnosia, 10
Follow-Through Program, 81
Frequency distribution curve, 7

Frustration, 14
  and curiosity, 55
  in mental retardation, 26
  and school curriculum, 26
  in sensory defects, 3, **4**
  and social promotion, 64
  due to visual or auditory handicap, 3
  due to writing difficulties, 15

G

Gaussian frequency distribution curve, 7
Genetic factors
  in Minimal Brain Dysfunction, 10
  in reading difficulties, 16-19
  in schizophrenia, 60
Gerstmann Syndrome, 10
Gifted children
  as underachievers, 30
Glandular malfunctions, 5
Glycoproteins, 73

H

Hallucinogenic drugs, 43
Handedness, determination of, 17
Handicap (*see* specific handicap)
Handwriting, poor, 15, 17
Head Start Program, 24, 25, 36, 81
Hereditary factors
  in reading problems, 19
Heterogeneous classes (grouping), 7, 63, 74
Hippie philosophy, 52
Homogeneous classes (grouping), 7, 8, 63
Hormonal influences, 73
Hostility, 12, 27
Hunger, 6
Hyperactive child (*see* Hyperkinetic and Overactive child)
Hyperkinesis (*see also* Minimal Brain Dysfunction), 8-17
  in schizophrenic child, 58

Hyperkinetic child
  and open-space classroom, 62-63
Hyperkinetic impulse disorder (*see* Minimal Brain Dysfunction)
Hyperkinetic syndrome (*see* Minimal Brain Dysfunction)
Hypoxia, 73

I

Identification, early, 19, 65, 66, 67, 80
Identity, changing, 60
Identity confusion, 49
Imipramine, 14
Impulse control, lack of, 10
Impulsive child (impulsivity), 8, 45
Individualization, 75
Individuation, 48
Industrialization, 76-78
Innate endowment
  as reflected in IQ, 23
Inner-drivenness, 11, 17
Insomnia
  due to stress, 44
Intellectual ability
  correlated with mental functioning, 22
Intellectual endowment, 23
Intellectual handicap, 65
Intellectual inadequacy, 26
Intellectual superiority
  relative, 29
  Intelligence Quotient, 22
  assessment of scores, 29
Intelligence tests, 22
  predictive value, 23

L

Language development, 7
Language difficulties, 17
Language therapy, 4, 15
Late bloomer, 64
Laterality, mixed, 17
Lead intoxication, 10

M

Malnutrition, 5, 73
Marital crisis
  affecting school performance, 45
Maturational lag, 6, 18
Maturational rates, 6, 7, 8
Meningitis, 10
Mental deficiency (*see* Mental
    retardation)
Mental retardation
  coexisting with dyslexia, 26
  mild, 25, 26
  and Minimal Brain Dysfunction, 8
  misdiagnosis in Minimal Brain
      Dysfunction, 58
  programs, 70
  relative, 26-28
Mentally retarded, educable (mild)
    classroom placement, 63
Methylphenidate, 14
Minimal brain damage (*see* Minimal
    Brain Dysfunction)
Minimal Brain Dysfunction, 8-16
  association with schizophrenia, 57-59
  and dyslexia, 67
  and educational deprivation, 29
  and hyperkinesis, 17
  and relative retardation, 28
Minimal cerebral dysfunction (*see*
    Minimal Brain Dysfunction)
Minimal chronic brain syndrome (*see*
    Minimal Brain Dysfunction)
Mixed laterality, 17
Mobility
  family, 32
  and wandering youth, 41
Mobility of population, 70
Mood alterators, 42
Motivation
  and child rearing practices, 80
  economic, 78
  and values, 41
Motivation, lack of, 51
  due to negative parental attitudes, 38
Motivation, low

due to environmental influences, 34,
    35
  in middle and upper classes, 36
Multidisciplinary approach, 13, 70
Multifactorial influences (causes), xi, 13
Multifactorial nature of handicap, 68

N

Nearsightedness, 6
Negativism, 54
Neurochemical disorders, 73
Neurological defects (deficits), 9, 10
Neurological signs, soft, 9
Neuromotor impairment, 8
Neurotic adaptive behavior, 33
Nutritional influences, 73

O

Obsessive-compulsive trends, 57
Open-spaced classrooms (schools), 9,
    14, 62, 63
Organic defects, ix
Organic drivenness, 9
Organic factors
  and maturation, 6
Organic impairment, 8
  (*see also* Minimal Brain Dysfunction)
Orthoptic training, 5
Overactivity, 11, 17

P

Parental neglect
  affecting school performance, 37
Penmanship, 15
Perinatal complications, 8
Perseveration, 8
Phobia, school, 48-51, 60
Physical defects
  leading to psychological stress, 47
Physical handicap, 3
  affecting academic performance, 29
Placebo-effect of medication, 14

Prevention, ix, x
  of deprivation, 24
  measures in, 80
  in Minimal Brain Dysfunction, 10
Primary reading retardation, 16
Projection, 56
Promotion, social, 64
Psychometric tests, 17
Psychosexual conflicts, 61
Psychosis (psychotic reaction), 28,
  57-61
Psychosomatic complaints (symptoms),
  34, 47
  and self-esteem, 33
  and separation anxiety, 50
Psychotherapy (*see* individual
  chapters)

R

Readiness levels, 7
Reading difficulties, 17
Reading disability
  in Japan, 79
Reading dysfunction, 5, 16
Reading readiness, 5, 7
  and school onset, 74, 75
Reading retardation, 19
Rebellion, 41, 54
Reciprocal effect
  of learning disorders and emotional
    factors, xi
Rejection, 51
Relevance, educational, 77
Remedial services, 80
Resources, educational, 78
Retardation (*see also* Mental
  retardation)
Retardation, academic, 51, 65
Reversal of letters, 7
Ritalin, 14

S

Schizophrenia, 51, 57-59
School phobia, 48, 49, 50, 60

Sedatives, 42
Self-concept
  and low achievement, 36
  of mother, 25
  of the retarded, 63
Self-confidence, 3
Self-esteem, 12
  affected by school difficulties, 44
  and cultural factors, 40
  and manual skills, 76
  and peer acceptance, 33
  low, 65
  low, and identity confusion, 49
Sensory deprivation, 4
Sensory handicap, 3
Separation, 48
  anxiety and school phobia, 50-51
  difficulties, 59
Sexual development, 46
Shyness, 6
Social pressure
  affecting school performance, 39
Social status, 76
Special classes, ungraded, 64
Specific developmental dyslexia, 16
Specific Reading Disability
    (Dysfunction), 17, 79
  and genetic factors, 16
  (*see also* Dyslexia)
Speech defects, 15
Speech development, 7
Speech problems, 17
Speech therapy, 4, 15
Spelling
  and simplification of language, 79
Stigmatization, 76, 80
Stimulant drugs, 14, 42
Stimulation, intellectual
  in high risk children, 80
  and intelligence, 23
Stimuli, auditory, 14
Stimuli, extraneous
  and distractibility, 9
  reduction of, 13
Stimuli, visual, 14
Stimulus deprivation, 4

Strabismus, 9
Strephosymbolia, 16
Stress
  in children with Minimal Brain
    Dysfunction, 59
  in major psychiatric disorders, 57
  psychological, 44
  psychological, due to physical
    conditions, 46
  as stimulus, 55
Suicidal attempt, suicide, 34, 49, 61
Syllabary system of writing, 20

T

Team approach, x
Team leader, 68, 70
Teamwork, 68
Tests, for early detection, 65-67
Therapy (*see* individual chapters)
Tranquilizers, 14
Treatment (*see* individual chapters)
Truancy, 51-53, 60
Twins, studies in reading problems, 19
Typewriter, use of, 15

U

Underachievement, 4, 64
Unwalled school (*see* Open spaced
    classroom)

V

Values, cultural
  and educational relevance, 76-78
Viral attacks, 73
Vision training, optometric, 4
Visual defects, handicap, 3, 6
Visual perceptual abilities, 4
Visual perceptual organization, 5
Visuomotor coordination, 17
Visuomotor discoordination, 8
Vocational choices, 76

W

Wandering youth, 41
Wechsler Inteligence Scale for
    Children, 17
Withdrawal, 4, 18
Withdrawn children, 65
Word blindness, 16